THE
TUNA FISH
GOURMET

▼▼▼▼▼

THE TUNA FISH GOURMET

▼▼▼▼▼

Tracey Seaman

DRAWINGS BY VICTORIA ROBERTS

A JOHN BOSWELL ASSOCIATES/
KING HILL PRODUCTIONS BOOK

Villard Books   New York 1994

I would like to thank:

Susan Wyler and the test kitchen and editorial staff at Food & Wine *magazine, especially Pamela Mitchell, Warren Picower and Tina Ujlaki, for their assistance.*

John Crowder from Pet Incorporated, Progresso Italian Foods, for his contribution.

The friends and relatives who inspired and supported me.

And mostly, my beloved tasters, Bob, Arnie and Lily, who ate more tuna fish than they ever dreamed possible.

Copyright © 1994 by John Boswell Management, Inc.

All rights reserved under International and Pan-American Copyright Conventions. Published in the United States by Villard Books, a division of Random House, Inc., New York and simultaneously in Canada by Random House of Canada Limited, Toronto.

Villard Books is a registered trademark of Random House, Inc.

Library of Congress Cataloging-in-Publication Data

Seaman, Tracey.
    The tuna fish gourmet / Tracey Seaman : drawings by Victoria Roberts.
        p.   cm.
    "A John Boswell Associates/King Hill Productions book."
    Includes index.
    ISBN: 0-679-75439-3
    It Cookery (Tuna)   I.   Title.   II.   Title: Tunafish gourmet.
TX748.T48S43   1994
641.6'92--dc20   93-40914
    ISBN 679-41878-4

Manufactured in the United States of America on acid-free paper

98765432

For
Lovey and Dad

CONTENTS
▼▼▼▼▼

Cold Appetizers and Snacks for Every Occasion—Whether you're sipping a martini or a hot cup of tea, Tuna-Mushroom Pâté, Rosy Avocado-Tuna Butter, Tuna Wraps with Peanut Sauce and Tuna and Black Olive Pinwheels are a sampling of the tasty nibbles.

Hot Hors d'Oeuvres and First Courses—On a serving tray, at the buffet table or in front of the VCR, recipes like Tuna-Stuffed Mushrooms, Tuna Ratatouille and Nachos with Tuna, Jalapeño Peppers and Cheese are sure to tempt the most discriminating guests and the fussiest kids.

Tuna Sandwiches and Melts—If there are any ideas you haven't thought of for sandwiching tuna, you'll find them here: Pita Pizza-Tuna Melt, Tuna Salad Siciliano, Tuna and Salad Pita Pockets and San Diego Melt with Avocado on Tortillas are just a few.

FOR TUNA LOVERS EVERYWHERE
▼▼▼▼▼

How many tuna salad sandwiches did you consume last month? If you are like millions of other Americans, the answer is at least one, and very possibly two a week. And that doesn't count tuna salad plates and tuna melts. Almost a billion pounds of canned tuna are consumed annually in the United States alone. Canned tuna is one of those exceptional foods that is convenient, tastes good and, unlike many other favorite treats, is actually very good for you.

For most of us, tuna fish is also the stuff of cozy childhood memories— Tuna Noodle Casserole, Creamed Tuna on Toast and, of course, zillions of tuna salad sandwiches on white bread, made with a generous helping of mayonnaise. That same tuna sandwich, embellished with chopped vegetables, fresh herbs, capers, olives, roasted peppers and the like, is still a staple in most of our adult diets. Only now it is just as likely to be spread between sourdough, seven-grain or French bread as between white or traditional rye.

Whether we make a sandwich ourselves and brown bag it, have the local coffee shop deliver one to our desks or order one at the local diner, tuna fish has a taste we never tire of. And cooks with young children know that along with peanut butter and jelly, it is one of the few foods almost universally enjoyed by the pickier culinary set.

Not only does canned tuna taste good, it is incredibly versatile. The tuna fish sandwich—with all its exciting combinations—is only the beginning. In *The Tuna Fish Gourmet*, tuna is also used as the starring ingredient in a variety of creative dishes: tuna with cocktails, tuna as a first course, tuna for a chic little luncheon and tuna for dinner. Some of those recipes are upscale and sophisticated; others are down-home and simply delicious. All are easy to make and fun to serve.

Beside fine flavor and convenience, tuna boasts an excellent nutritional profile. Tuna fish contains only 111 calories per 3-ounce serving if purchased packed in water. Tuna in oil, drained, contains 168 calories. It is high in protein, niacin, vitamins B6 and B12, vitamin D and phosphorus. In addition, tuna is rich in omega-3 oils, which some doctors believe may help to guard against cholesterol buildup and cardiovascular disease.

One of the great appeals of cooking with tuna fish is the fact that it comes in a can. While you are reaching for something to make at the last minute for a quick and easy meal, tasty tuna is sitting in the cupboard, ready whenever you are. These days, most tuna comes in 6⅛-ounce or 6½-ounce cans; these sizes can be used interchangeably.

A NOTE ABOUT THE RECIPES: Each recipe specifies a particular type of tuna. These designations simply mean that the specific kind of tuna recommended was my favorite when tested in that recipe and is the best possible variety for that particular dish. My own personal preference is solid white, rather than chunk light, because it is firmer and milder. Of course, any kind of tuna that you like can be used in any recipe. Tuna packed in olive oil has a little more flavor than tuna packed in vegetable oil, but they are virtually interchangeable. Tuna packed in water is a bit drier, but many people who are eating lighter prefer it, and it can be substituted in any of these recipes with perfectly satisfactory results.

A NOTE ABOUT TUNA FISHING AND DOLPHINS: All domestically packed tuna fish in the United States is dolphin safe by law. That means the nets used to catch the fish are employed in ways that do not encircle and trap dolphins. Laws in other countries vary. To make sure you are purchasing dolphin-safe tuna, look for the special symbol on the label.

CHAPTER 1
▼▼▼▼▼
TUNA WITH COCKTAILS

ROSY AVOCADO-TUNA BUTTER

TUNA-MUSHROOM PÂTÉ

TUNA TAPENADE

CREAMY TUNA DIP WITH CRUNCHY ONIONS

ANTIPASTO FOR FOUR

TUNA AND COTTAGE CHEESE SPREAD WITH HORSERADISH

TUNA COCKTAIL

TUNA-STUFFED CUCUMBER CUPS

TUNA BRUSCHETTA WITH RADICCHIO, CURRANTS AND PINE NUTS

RIBBON SANDWICHES

CHECKERBOARD SANDWICHES

TUNA WRAPS WITH PEANUT SAUCE

TUNA AND BLACK OLIVE PINWHEELS

TUNA TRIANGLES WITH CUCUMBER AND DILL

ROSY AVOCADO-
TUNA BUTTER
▼▼▼▼▼

Here's a spread that you can serve on toasted baguette slices as well as on grilled chicken. It will keep for up to a week in the refrigerator. Let soften at room temperature for 30 minutes before serving.

MAKES ABOUT 1½ CUPS

1 stick (4 ounces) cold unsalted butter

1 (6⅛-ounce) can solid white tuna in water, drained

½ ripe avocado, peeled and pitted

1 tablespoon fresh lime juice

½ cup roasted red pepper strips, fresh or jarred

2 tablespoons chopped fresh parsley

½ teaspoon freshly ground black pepper

¼ teaspoon salt

1. In a food processor, combine the butter, tuna and avocado. Puree until smooth, about 15 seconds. Add the lime juice and process for 10 seconds, scraping down the sides as needed until blended.

2. Add the red pepper strips, parsley, pepper and salt and pulse until the mixture has tiny flecks of red and green. Serve immediately or cover and refrigerate.

TUNA-MUSHROOM PÂTÉ
▼▼▼▼▼

If you're in a hurry, serve this spread in a bowl as soon as it is made. For a more decorative presentation, line a 2-cup mold or terrine with a large sheet of plastic wrap, scoop the pâté inside, smooth the top, fold over the wrap and refrigerate until chilled, about 2 hours. Unwrap the pâté, invert onto a plate and serve with toast points, toasted baguette slices or melba toast.

MAKES ABOUT 2 CUPS

10 ounces medium mushrooms
2 tablespoons unsalted butter
¼ teaspoon dried thyme
¼ cup chopped onion
2 garlic cloves, chopped
2 tablespoons dry sherry
1 (6½-ounce) can tuna in olive oil, drained
¼ cup cream cheese
¼ teaspoon freshly ground black pepper
Pinch of salt

1. Place the mushrooms in a food processor and pulse about 8 times to coarsely chop. Melt the butter in a heavy medium skillet over moderately high heat. Add the chopped mushrooms and cook, stirring, until they begin to brown, about 5 minutes. Stir in the thyme, onion and garlic, reduce the heat to moderately low and cook, stirring often, for about 3 minutes, until the onions are soft and the mushroom juices have evaporated. Add the sherry and cook, stirring, until evaporated, 1 to 2 minutes. Remove from the heat and let cool for 10 minutes.

2. Transfer the mushroom mixture to the food processor. Add the tuna, cream cheese, pepper and salt. Process until blended to a coarse puree, about 10 seconds. Serve as indicated above.

▼ THE TUNA FISH GOURMET ▼

5

TUNA TAPENADE

▼▼▼▼▼

Many people have tasted tapenade made with olives, but the tuna version given here is just as authentic. The tart spread is good on plain French bread, garlic bagel chips or crackers. For a truly Mediterranean touch, try the garlic toasts suggested below.

MAKES 1 CUP

1 (6⅛-ounce) can tuna in olive oil, drained

1 garlic clove, peeled

1 tablespoon fresh lemon juice

¼ teaspoon freshly ground black pepper

1 tablespoon chopped fresh parsley

3 tablespoons olive oil, preferably extra-virgin

1 tablespoon capers in vinegar, rinsed

Garlic Toasts (recipe follows)

1. Place the tuna, garlic, lemon juice, pepper and parsley in a food processor. Turn the machine on and slowly pour the olive oil through the feed tube.

2. Stop the machine and scrape down the sides. Add the capers and pulse briefly to chop them into the mixture. Scrape the tapenade into a small serving bowl, cover and refrigerate until ready to use. Serve with the garlic toasts on the side.

GARLIC TOASTS

MAKES 8

8 (or more) diagonal slices Italian bread, about ⅜ inch
   thick
Olive oil, for brushing
1 garlic clove, cut in half

1. Preheat the oven to 375° Place the bread slices on a small baking sheet and brush lightly with olive oil Bake for 8 to 10 minutes, until golden brown and crisp.

2. Remove from the oven and rub immediately with the cut side of the garlic.

CREAMY TUNA DIP WITH CRUNCHY ONIONS

▼▼▼▼▼

I highly recommend eating this dip with potato chips (remember tuna fish and chip sandwiches?), but it also goes well with assorted fresh veggies. Note the options of using reduced-fat cream cheese and sour cream for fewer calories and less cholesterol.

MAKES ABOUT 2½ CUPS

12 ounces cream cheese or Neufchâtel (1½ large
   packages)

½ cup sour cream

1 (6⅛-ounce) can solid white tuna in water, well
   drained

2 tablespoons minced fresh chives

¼ teaspoon freshly ground black pepper

2 cups vegetable oil, for frying

1 medium onion, peeled, halved and thinly sliced

¼ cup all-purpose flour

⅛ teaspoon salt

1. Place the cream cheese, sour cream and tuna in a food processor Puree until smooth, about 20 seconds, scraping down the side of the bowl several times.

2. Add the chives and pepper and process briefly to blend. Scrape into a crock or medium bowl, cover and refrigerate. (The recipe can be prepared to this point 1 day ahead.)

3. Heat the oil in a medium saucepan over moderately high heat to 350° Meanwhile, toss the onion slices with the flour and salt to coat well. Shake off the excess. Fry the onions until crisp and golden, about 2 minutes. Remove with a slotted spoon, drain on paper towels and let cool. (The onions can be fried 1 day ahead and stored in an airtight container. In cases of high humidity, re-crisp the onions if necessary in a 400° oven.) Crumble the onions over the crock of dip and serve.

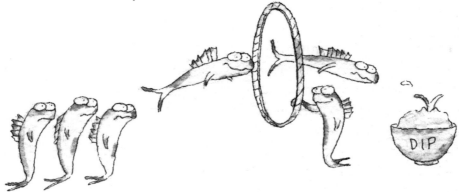

▼ THE TUNA FISH GOURMET ▼

ANTIPASTO FOR FOUR

▼▼▼▼▼

For entertaining, assemble this platter of assorted appetizers one hour ahead. Use any or all of the elements listed here or add your own ideas. You can even make a meal out of it. Serve with several types of crusty bread.

MAKES 4 SERVINGS

1 small eggplant (about ¾ pound), cut crosswise on the
   diagonal into ¼-inch-thick slices
1 small zucchini, cut crosswise on the diagonal into
   ¼-inch-thick slices
8 medium mushrooms, stemmed
3 tablespoons olive oil
1½ tablespoons fresh lemon juice
½ teaspoon freshly ground black pepper
Sun-dried tomatoes, packed in oil
1 (6½-ounce) can tuna in olive oil, drained
4 paper-thin slices of prosciutto
Roasted red peppers, cut into 1-inch strips
Sliced aged Provolone cheese
Anchovies

1. Prepare a grill or heat the broiler. Place the eggplant and zucchini slices and the mushroom caps on a tray and lightly brush with the olive oil. Sprinkle the lemon juice over the vegetables and season with the pepper.

2. Grill or broil the vegetables until charred and softened, 6 to 8 minutes, turning once or twice. The timing will depend on the intensity of the heat. Remove from the heat and let cool.

3. Arrange the grilled vegetables and the remaining ingredients on a platter and serve with drinks as lunch or as an element of a buffet.

TUNA AND COTTAGE CHEESE SPREAD WITH HORSERADISH

▼▼▼▼▼

Serve with bagel chips or melba rounds and sesame bread sticks. This also makes a great topping for baked potatoes.

MAKES ABOUT 2 CUPS

1 (6⅛-ounce) can solid white tuna in water, drained
   and finely flaked
1½ cups cottage cheese
¼ teaspoon freshly ground black pepper
1 to 2 tablespoons prepared white horseradish, or to
   taste
1 scallion green, finely chopped

Place all of the ingredients in a medium bowl and stir to blend. Use at once or cover and refrigerate for up to 2 days before serving.

TUNA COCKTAIL

▼▼▼▼▼

Tuna goes Southwestern in this easy appetizer—a great quick fix to serve with drinks. Use the best-quality salsa you can find in your local market.

MAKES ABOUT 8 SERVINGS

1 (8-ounce) package cream cheese, slightly softened
1 (6⅛-ounce) can solid white tuna in oil or water,
  drained and flaked
½ cup mild salsa
Water crackers or tortilla chips, for serving

Smear the cream cheese over the bottom of a 7-inch shallow bowl or an 8-inch oval gratin. Spoon the flaked tuna evenly over the cheese. Spoon the salsa on top. Serve immediately, with water crackers or tortilla chips.

TUNA-STUFFED
CUCUMBER CUPS
▼▼▼▼▼

For variety, try the tuna filling in this recipe (step 1) as a spread on crackers or use celery sticks in place of the cucumber cups.

MAKES 2 DOZEN

1 (8-ounce) package cream cheese

2 ounces blue cheese, preferably Danish blue

2 tablespoons mayonnaise

1 (3-ounce) can tuna in oil, drained

¼ to ½ teaspoon freshly ground black pepper

1 European or hothouse cucumber, peeled and cut into
   24 slices ½ inch thick

¼ cup minced fresh chives, for garnish

1. Place the cream cheese, blue cheese, mayonnaise, tuna and pepper in a food processor. Puree until well blended and relatively smooth, about 30 seconds; scrape down the sides of the bowl as necessary.

2. With a melon baller, gently hollow out the seedy center area of each cucumber slice about halfway down, leaving a bottom.

3. Spoon (or pipe) a rounded teaspoon of the tuna mixture into each of the cucumber cups. Garnish each with a sprinkling of chives. Arrange on a platter and serve. (The recipe can be prepared about 1 hour ahead; cover loosely and chill until ready to serve.)

TUNA BRUSCHETTA WITH RADICCHIO, CURRANTS AND PINE NUTS

▼▼▼▼▼

Here's a recipe that could be direct from the toniest trattoria in Manhattan or L.A. Canned tuna fish is combined with radicchio—an Italian lettuce that is all the rage for its lovely purplish red color and mildly bitter flavor—sweet currants and aromatic toasted pine nuts. The whole is tossed with a savory vinaigrette and piled on slices of good garlic bread.

MAKES 6 APPETIZER SERVINGS

¼ cup currants

½ cup boiling water

¼ cup pine nuts (about 1 ounce)

1 (6½-ounce) can tuna in olive oil, drained and flaked

½ medium head of radicchio, cored and thinly sliced
   into shreds

2 teaspoons red wine vinegar

1 teaspoon Dijon mustard

1 teaspoon anchovy paste

2 tablespoons extra-virgin olive oil

½ teaspoon freshly ground black pepper

6 slices of large Italian bread, such as peasant or
   semolina, about 3 by 7 inches, cut ½ inch thick

1 large garlic clove, halved

1. Place the currants in a small bowl. Add the boiling water and let soak for about 15 minutes until plumped. Drain well.

2. Meanwhile, place the pine nuts in a small, dry skillet over moderately low heat. Cook, shaking the pan occasionally, until the nuts are golden and fragrant, 4 to 6 minutes.

3. Transfer the currants and pine nuts to a medium bowl. Add the tuna and shredded radicchio and toss to mix. In a small bowl, whisk together the vinegar, mustard and anchovy paste. Slowly drizzle in the oil, whisking until incorporated. Stir in the pepper. Toss the dressing with the tuna mixture.

4. Toast the bread slices and lightly rub on one side with the cut garlic clove. Place about ⅓ cup of the tuna and radicchio mixture on top of each toast. Serve immediately.

RIBBON SANDWICHES

▼▼▼▼▼

Stripes of light and dark bread alternate with a tasty tuna filling flecked with green chives to create an attractive choice for a party platter or buffet table. These dainty sandwiches can be made with a variety of salad fillings. Cut the fingers in half to make smaller, square sandwiches if you prefer.

MAKES 18 FINGER SANDWICHES

1 (6⅛-ounce) can solid white tuna in oil,
   drained and flaked
2 tablespoons mayonnaise
2 teaspoons fresh lemon juice
¼ teaspoon freshly ground black pepper
2 tablespoons minced fresh chives
6 slices of firm-textured white bread
6 slices of firm-textured whole wheat bread

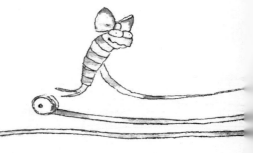

1. In a food processor, combine the tuna, mayonnaise, lemon juice and pepper. Process until relatively smooth, scraping down the sides once or twice, about 30 seconds. Add the chives and pulse briefly to combine. Transfer to a small bowl.

2. Spread 1 rounded tablespoon of the tuna mixture on 4 of the white bread slices and 4 of the whole wheat slices. Pile them up, alternating wheat and white and top with a contrasting slice of plain bread. There will be 3 stacked sandwiches. (The recipe can be made to this point up to several hours ahead; wrap and refrigerate.)

3. Using a serrated knife, remove the crusts, then cut each sandwich into 6 slices ½ inch wide. Arrange on a tray and serve.

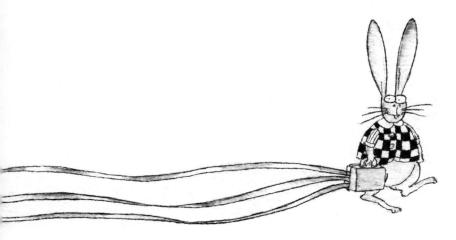

▼ THE TUNA FISH GOURMET ▼

CHECKERBOARD
SANDWICHES
▼▼▼▼▼

Here is another decorative idea, which takes ribbon sandwiches a step further. A yellow and white egg salad adds variety and color interest. If you prefer to use more tuna instead of the egg, make a second batch of the tuna from step 1 of the Ribbon Sandwiches. Instead of the chives, substitute 2 tablespoons of finely chopped roasted red peppers.

MAKES 36 BITE-SIZED FINGER SANDWICHES

1 recipe Ribbon Sandwiches (page 18)

4 large eggs

3 tablespoons mayonnaise

1 teaspoon Dijon mustard

¼ teaspoon salt

¼ teaspoon freshly ground black pepper

1. Make the ribbon sandwiches; cover and refrigerate. Place the eggs in a medium saucepan with salted water to cover. Bring to a boil over moderately high heat. Reduce the heat slightly and boil gently for 10 minutes. Drain and add several changes of cold water to the pot until the eggs are cool. Peel, rinse and quarter the hard-cooked eggs.

2. Place the quartered eggs in the food processor and pulse about 3 times, until coarsely chopped. Add the mayonnaise, mustard, salt and pepper and process until just combined; there should be bits of egg white visible. Transfer to a medium bowl.

3. Spread 1 tablespoon of the egg salad onto each of 6 slices of the ribbon sandwiches that are topped with white bread, smoothing to cover evenly. Spread 1 tablespoon of the egg salad onto each of 6 of the whole wheat-topped ribbon sandwiches. Stack the sandwiches in 2 layers, making 3 stacks with the white on top and 3 with the wheat on top. Cover with the remaining 6 sandwiches to make a third layer, again alternating the colors of bread. There will be 6 sandwich stacks with 3 layers to a stack. Wrap each section separately in waxed paper and refrigerate for 1 hour, or overnight.

4. When ready to serve, use a serrated knife to slice each stack crosswise into 6 small, square finger sandwiches. Arrange on a tray and serve.

TUNA WRAPS WITH PEANUT SAUCE

▼▼▼▼▼

These hand-held tuna treats were inspired by Marcia Kiesel, my friend and colleague, who has an abiding love for Vietnamese food. They make a great party snack or sandwich substitute.

MAKES 2 SERVINGS

2 tablespoons creamy peanut butter

½ teaspoon minced garlic

2 teaspoons soy sauce

1 teaspoon Asian sesame oil

1 teaspoon fresh lemon juice

4 large leaves of Boston lettuce

1⅓ cups bean sprouts

8 thin red or green bell pepper strips, about
    2 inches long

1 (6⅛-ounce) can solid white tuna in oil, drained
    and lightly flaked

1 large carrot, peeled and shredded

4 sprigs of fresh cilantro

1. In a small bowl, whisk together the peanut butter, garlic, soy sauce, sesame oil, lemon juice and 2 teaspoons of water until well blended. Set the sauce aside.

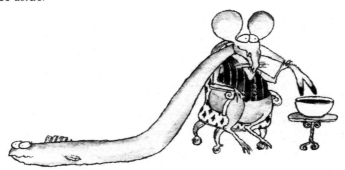

2. Lay the lettuce leaves on a flat work surface. Place ⅓ cup of the bean sprouts on top of each, leaving almost a 1-inch border. Lay 2 pepper strips side by side vertically in the center over the sprouts; then mound one-fourth of the tuna down the center over the peppers. Drizzle one-fourth of the sauce over each mound of tuna. Distribute the carrot over the tuna; then top each portion with a sprig of cilantro.

3. To roll up, begin at one side, roll across to the other and enjoy.

TUNA AND BLACK OLIVE PINWHEELS

▼▼▼▼▼

Spiral sandwiches look complicated, but they are easy to construct if you can find a loaf of unsliced white bread. Most bakeries sell them, sometimes under the name "pullman loaf."

MAKES 20 FINGER SANDWICHES

1 (1-pound) loaf of *unsliced* firm-textured white bread

1 (6½-ounce) can tuna, preferably in olive oil, drained

3 tablespoons mayonnaise

2 tablespoons cream cheese

¼ teaspoon freshly ground black pepper

¼ cup lightly packed Italian parsley

2 tablespoons chopped, pitted, oil-cured Italian
   black olives

1. With a large serrated knife, cut the crust off one long side of the bread. Then cut 4 lengthwise slices about ⅜ inch thick. Reserve the remaining loaf for another use.

2. In a food processor, combine the tuna, mayonnaise, cream cheese, pepper and parsley. Process to blend, scraping down the bowl once, to make a coarse puree, about 10 seconds. Transfer to a medium bowl and stir in the chopped olives.

3. With a serrated knife, cut the crusts off the short ends of the bread. Spread one-fourth of the tuna mixture over one of the bread slices. Roll up the bread from one short end to the other. Repeat with the remaining slices and tuna mixture. Wrap the rolls in waxed paper and refrigerate for up to 3 hours.

4. Unwrap the rolls and, using the serrated knife, remove the crust ends. Then slice each roll into 5 pinwheels about ½ inch wide. Arrange on a tray and serve.

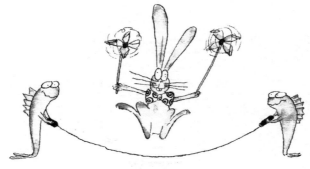

▼ THE TUNA FISH GOURMET ▼

TUNA TRIANGLES WITH CUCUMBER AND DILL

▼▼▼▼▼

A hint of lime lends a refreshing twist to these charming little sandwiches.

MAKES 20 SMALL SANDWICHES

2 (6⅛-ounce) cans solid white tuna in water, drained
   and flaked
½ cup finely chopped peeled and seeded cucumber
¼ teaspoon freshly ground black pepper
1½ tablespoons finely chopped fresh dill
⅓ cup plus about ¾ cup mayonnaise, for coating the
   sides of the sandwiches
1 tablespoon fresh lime juice
20 slices of firm-textured white bread, crusts removed
1 cup finely chopped fresh parsley

1. In a medium bowl, combine the tuna, cucumber, pepper and dill. Mix with a fork. Stir in ⅓ cup mayonnaise and the lime juice until well blended.

2. Lay 5 slices of the bread on a flat work surface. Spread about ¼ cup of the tuna mixture over each and cover with 5 of the remaining bread slices. Set aside and repeat with the remaining bread and tuna mixture.

3. With a serrated knife, cut the sandwiches in half diagonally. Place the parsley in a wide shallow bowl or plate. Spread about 2 teaspoons of mayonnaise all the way around the cut sides of one of the sandwiches, then dip the coated edges into the parsley to coat the edges lightly. Shake gently to remove any excess. Repeat with the remaining sandwiches and parsley.

4. Arrange the triangles on a platter and serve immediately, or cover with a damp cloth and then with plastic wrap and refrigerate for up to 3 hours before serving.

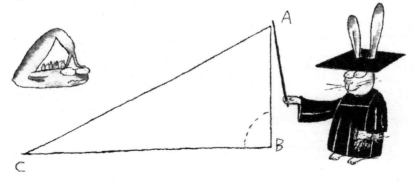

▼ THE TUNA FISH GOURMET ▼

CHAPTER 2

▼▼▼▼▼

HOT STARTERS

MINI MELTS WITH CHEDDAR AND PAN-FRIED ONIONS
TUNA-STUFFED MUSHROOMS
GOLDEN TUNA COINS
TUNA "LATKES"
TUNA RATATOUILLE
NACHOS WITH TUNA, JALAPEÑO PEPPERS AND CHEESE
HOT TUNA SPREAD

MINI MELTS WITH CHEDDAR AND PAN-FRIED ONIONS

▼▼▼▼▼

Browned onions turn an ordinary melt into an irresistible treat. This is a pretty substantial appetizer, appropriate to pass as a hot hors d'oeuvre; it also makes a great snack.

MAKES 8 MINI OPEN-FACE SANDWICHES

8 slices of party pumpernickel or rye bread

1 (6⅛-ounce) can solid white tuna in water, drained
   and lightly flaked

2 tablespoons mayonnaise

¼ teaspoon plus a pinch of freshly ground black pepper

½ tablespoon unsalted butter

1 medium onion, halved and very thinly sliced

Pinch of dried thyme

Pinch of salt

½ cup lightly packed, grated extra sharp white Cheddar
   cheese (about 3 ounces)

▼ THE TUNA FISH GOURMET ▼

1. Preheat the broiler. Place the slices of party bread on a small baking sheet and set aside until ready to broil.

2. In a medium bowl, combine the tuna, mayonnaise and ¼ teaspoon pepper. Stir with a fork until blended. Cover and refrigerate.

3. Heat a heavy medium skillet over moderately high heat until hot but not smoking, about 2 minutes. Add the butter and, when melted, the onions. Cook the onions, stirring occasionally, until nicely browned, about 4 minutes. Reduce the heat to low, add the thyme and a pinch of salt and pepper and continue to cook for 2 minutes longer, until the onions are very soft. Remove from the heat.

4. Place the prepared baking sheet under the hot broiler 4 to 6 inches from the heat and toast the bread lightly on the top side, about 2 minutes. Remove from the oven. Turn the slices over and top each with 1 rounded tablespoon of the tuna mixture. Distribute the browned onions over the tuna and top each with 1 tablespoon of the grated cheese. Broil about 1 minute, until the cheese is melted. Serve immediately.

TUNA-STUFFED
MUSHROOMS
▼▼▼▼▼

A little tuna goes a long way as it's used here in place of expensive crabmeat. Because the mushrooms can be stuffed up to a day ahead and baked at the last moment, this is a time-saving recipe for entertaining.

MAKES ABOUT 18

10 ounces medium white mushrooms

1 tablespoon unsalted butter

1 tablespoon olive oil

¼ cup minced onion

¼ teaspoon dried thyme

¼ teaspoon freshly ground black pepper

2 tablespoons dry vermouth or sherry

1 (3-ounce) can solid white tuna in oil or water, drained

¼ cup plain dry bread crumbs

1 tablespoon grated Parmesan cheese

1. Remove the stems from the mushrooms and finely chop them. Reserve the caps. In a medium skillet, melt the butter in the oil over moderately high heat. Add the chopped mushroom stems and cook, stirring often, until nicely browned, about 5 minutes. Reduce the heat to moderately low, add the onion, thyme and pepper and cook for 2 minutes longer.

2. Stir in the vermouth and cook until evaporated, about 1 minute. Scrape into a medium bowl. With a fork, stir in the tuna, bread crumbs and 1 tablespoon of water. Blend in the Parmesan cheese.

3. Stuff the mushroom caps firmly with the filling, rounding the tops slightly. (The recipe can be made up to 1 day ahead; cover and refrigerate.)

4. When ready to serve, preheat the oven to 400°. Place the stuffed mushrooms on a baking sheet and bake for about 15 minutes, until hot and golden brown on top.

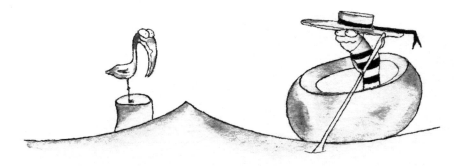

▼ THE TUNA FISH GOURMET ▼

GOLDEN TUNA COINS

▼▼▼▼▼

A crispy coated hors d'oeuvre best served with a simple cocktail sauce of ketchup, plenty of horseradish and some fresh lemon juice. When increasing the recipe, use a larger pan or cook in batches.

MAKES ABOUT 7 COINS, 2 TO 3 SERVINGS

1 (6⅛-ounce) can solid white tuna in oil, drained and flaked

¼ teaspoon dried thyme

2 tablespoons mayonnaise

½ teaspoon freshly ground black pepper

¼ cup all-purpose flour

⅛ teaspoon salt

1 egg

2 tablespoons yellow cornmeal

2 tablespoons plain dry bread crumbs

3 tablespoons corn oil, for frying

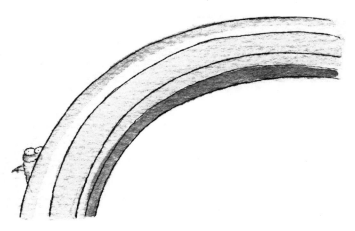

1. In a small bowl, mix together the tuna, thyme, mayonnaise and ¼ teaspoon of the pepper with a fork until blended.

2. Place the flour, half the salt and the remaining ¼ teaspoon pepper on a medium plate and toss to combine. Dust your hands with the mixture and, measuring out heaping tablespoons of the tuna mixture, form about 7 patties 1½ inches in diameter. Coat them well with the seasoned flour.

3. In a shallow bowl, beat the egg until blended. In another bowl, toss together the cornmeal, bread crumbs and remaining salt. Turn the patties in the beaten egg, then coat well in the crumbs.

4. Heat a medium skillet, preferably cast-iron, over moderate heat. When hot, add the oil. Carefully place the patties in the pan and fry until browned and crisp, about 1 minute per side. Serve immediately.

TUNA "LATKES"

▼▼▼▼▼

Since these potato pancakes cook in three batches and should be brought to the table piping hot, keep them in a low oven on a rack on a baking sheet until ready to serve.

MAKES 6 SIDE-DISH OR APPETIZER SERVINGS

1 medium onion, grated

2 large baking potatoes (about 1 pound total), peeled
  and grated

1 (6⅛-ounce) can solid white tuna in oil, drained

2 eggs, beaten

½ teaspoon salt

½ teaspoon freshly ground black pepper

Vegetable oil, for pan frying

Sour cream and minced fresh chives, as
  accompaniments

1. Spread the grated onion and potatoes on a clean kitchen towel. Roll up the towel, then squeeze and wring out as much liquid as possible.

2. Transfer the onion and potatoes to a large bowl. Stir in the tuna, beaten eggs, salt and pepper.

3. Heat a heavy large skillet over moderately high heat for 2 to 3 minutes, until almost smoking. Add about 3 tablespoons of oil, let heat, then drop in about 6 heaping tablespoons of the potato-tuna mixture, about 2 inches apart. Flatten slightly with a wide spatula to make 2-inch pancakes and cook, turning once, about 2½ minutes per side, until crisp and well browned. Drain on paper towels. Continue cooking the rest of the pancakes the same way. Sprinkle the pancakes lightly with additional salt to taste. Top with a dab of sour cream and a sprinkling of chives and serve immediately

TUNA RATATOUILLE

▼▼▼▼▼

Here's a crowd-pleasing spread for garlic toasts (page 7) or crackers. For a main course, the hot ratatouille can be tossed with a pound of pasta. At any temperature, it makes a fine side dish with meat or fish.

MAKES ABOUT 5 CUPS

2 large eggplants (about 1½ pounds each), trimmed and
    halved lengthwise
¼ cup plus 1 tablespoon olive oil, mild or extra-virgin
1 medium zucchini, trimmed and cut into ¼-inch dice
1 medium onion, finely chopped
2 large garlic cloves, finely chopped
1 medium red bell pepper, cut into ¼-inch dice
½ cup dry white wine
2 teaspoons chopped fresh oregano or 1 teaspoon dried
½ teaspoon salt
½ teaspoon freshly ground black pepper
4 fresh plum tomatoes, cut into ¼-inch dice
2 (6⅛-ounce) cans tuna in olive oil, drained and flaked
⅓ cup capers, rinsed and drained

1. Preheat the oven to 350°. Brush the cut sides of the eggplants with about 1 tablespoon of the olive oil and place cut side down on a large baking sheet. Place in the oven and bake for 1 hour, or until soft when pierced with a fork.

2. While the eggplants are cooking, heat the remaining ¼ cup olive oil in a large skillet over moderately low heat. Add the zucchini, onion, garlic and red bell pepper. Cook, stirring often, until the onion is translucent, about 6 minutes. Stir in the white wine, oregano, salt and pepper and continue cooking until the vegetables are soft and the wine has evaporated, 10 to 12 minutes longer. Remove from the heat.

3. When the eggplants have finished roasting, transfer to a paper bag and let cool for about 15 minutes.

4. Peel off the skin and chop the eggplant with a large sharp knife. Stir into the other cooked vegetables in the skillet and place over moderately high heat. Cook, stirring occasionally, until hot, 3 to 4 minutes. Stir in the chopped tomatoes, tuna and capers and cook 2 minutes longer. Season with additional salt and pepper to taste. Scrape into a large crock or bowl and serve hot, warm or at room temperature.

NACHOS WITH TUNA, JALAPEÑO PEPPERS AND CHEESE

▼▼▼▼▼

While I've called for a moderate topping of chiles here, add more or less depending on how hot you like it. Serve the nachos with sour cream and guacamole, or warm refried beans.

MAKES 2 TO 4 SERVINGS

Tortilla chips, lightly salted or unsalted

½ cup lightly packed, grated extra sharp Cheddar
  cheese (about 3 ounces)

1 (6⅛-ounce) can solid white tuna in oil, drained and
  well flaked

½ cup grated Monterey jack cheese (about 3 ounces)

1 tablespoon chopped pickled jalapeño peppers or
  chopped green chiles

1 ripe medium tomato, seeded and finely diced

1. Arrange a rack 6 to 8 inches from the heat and preheat the broiler. On a 10-by-15-inch jelly-roll pan or baking sheet with sides, arrange a single layer of tortilla chips, overlapping slightly, leaving as little space as possible in between.

2. Evenly distribute the Cheddar cheese over the top and then the tuna. Sprinkle on the Monterey jack, then the jalapeños and the tomato. Place in the oven and broil until the cheese is melted and the chips are hot, about 5 minutes, turning the pan as necessary for even cooking. Serve immediately.

HOT TUNA SPREAD

▼▼▼▼▼

Serve on crackers or toast points or use as a topping for baked potatoes.

MAKES ABOUT 2 CUPS

4 ounces cream cheese (½ large package), softened
1 (6⅛-ounce) can solid white tuna in oil or water,
    drained and flaked
3 tablespoons mayonnaise
½ cup grated imported Swiss cheese (about 3 ounces)
¼ teaspoon freshly ground black pepper
2 tablespoons plain dry bread crumbs

1. Preheat the oven to 400°. In a medium bowl, combine the cream cheese, tuna, mayonnaise, grated cheese and pepper. Blend well.

2. Scrape the tuna mixture into a soup crock or small (1 pint) ovenproof casserole. Sprinkle the bread crumbs over the top. Bake for about 20 minutes, until golden brown and bubbly.

CHAPTER 3

BETWEEN THE BREAD

NAKED TUNA SALAD

HERBED TUNA SALAD

CONFETTI TUNA SALAD

TUNA SALAD SICILIANO

TUNA AND EGG SALAD

TUNA AND SALAD PITA POCKETS

TUNA AND MARMALADE ON TOAST

LIGHT TUNA SALAD WITH LEMON AND RELISH

TUNA CLUB #1

TUNA CLUB #2

CLASSIC TUNA MELT

PITA PIZZA-TUNA MELT

SAN DIEGO MELT WITH AVOCADO ON TORTILLAS

TUNA MELT WITH BACON AND SWISS CHEESE

TUNA "CROQUE"

BAGEL MELT

SEMOLINA MELT

NAKED TUNA SALAD

▼▼▼▼▼

This, and the following half dozen tuna salad recipes, can be incorporated into sandwiches, melts and more complex salads. Since the texture of tuna salad is quite personal, do as you wish to flake the fish until it is as coarse or fine as you like.

MAKES 1⅔ CUPS, ENOUGH FOR 4 SANDWICHES
OR SALAD PLATES

2 (6⅛-ounce) cans solid white tuna in oil or water,
   drained and flaked
¼ cup mayonnaise
Freshly ground black pepper

Combine all of the ingredients in a medium bowl. Blend with a fork. Chill if desired.

HERBED TUNA SALAD

▼▼▼▼▼

This versatile tuna mixture is my friend Susan Brennan's favorite. Fresh dill, chives or parsley can be substituted for the thyme. Use for any melt or as a filling for avocado halves.

MAKES 2 CUPS

2 (6⅛-ounce) cans solid white tuna in water, drained
   and flaked
3 tablespoons mayonnaise
1 medium celery rib, finely diced
1 scallion, finely chopped
1 tablespoon fresh lemon juice
1 teaspoon finely chopped fresh thyme leaves
Freshly ground black pepper

Combine all of the ingredients in a medium bowl. Mix with a fork until well blended. Chill if desired.

CONFETTI TUNA SALAD

▼▼▼▼▼

Flecks of red and green bell peppers add a festive touch while they also contribute sweetness and a little crunch.

MAKES 2 CUPS

2 (6⅛-ounce) cans solid white tuna in oil, drained and
   flaked
3 tablespoons mayonnaise
1 teaspoon fresh lime juice
1 tablespoon minced fresh chives
¼ cup finely diced red bell pepper
2 tablespoons finely diced green bell pepper

Combine all of the ingredients in a medium bowl. Mix with a fork until well blended. Chill if desired.

TUNA SALAD SICILIANO

▼▼▼▼▼

Spread this salad on thin slices of crusty peasant bread or sandwich between a split piece of focaccia or an English muffin. Black olives can be substituted for the green. It is also a good choice to use on the Semolina Melt on page 69.

MAKES ABOUT 1⅓ CUPS

1 (6½-ounce) can tuna in olive oil, drained and flaked
4 sun-dried tomatoes, packed in oil, cut into thin strips
¼ cup finely chopped pitted green olives
1 medium celery rib, thinly sliced
1 tablespoon olive oil
1 teaspoon red wine vinegar
½ teaspoon freshly ground black pepper

In a medium bowl, toss together the tuna, sun-dried tomato strips, olives and celery. Drizzle on the oil and toss to incorporate; then toss with the vinegar and pepper.

TUNA AND EGG SALAD

▼▼▼▼▼

Serve this old favorite on soft whole wheat bread with sliced tomatoes and alfalfa sprouts.

MAKES ABOUT 1¼ CUPS, ENOUGH FOR
2 SANDWICHES OR STUFFED TOMATOES

2 large eggs
Pinch of salt
1 (6⅛-ounce) can solid white tuna in water, drained
   and flaked
2 tablespoons mayonnaise
½ teaspoon freshly ground black pepper
1 tablespoon minced fresh chives

1. Place the eggs in a medium saucepan with water to cover and add the salt. Bring to a boil over moderately high heat. Reduce the heat to moderate and boil gently for 10 minutes. Drain and add cold running water to the pot. Let the eggs sit in the cold water until cool. (You may need to add several changes of cold water.)

2. Peel the eggs and finely chop. Place in a medium bowl and toss with the tuna. Stir in the mayonnaise, pepper and chives. Season with additional salt to taste.

▼ THE TUNA FISH GOURMET ▼

TUNA AND SALAD PITA POCKETS

▼▼▼▼▼

Instead of the usual iceberg lettuce, try one of the varieties suggested. Tender greens pack nicely in the soft pita bread.

MAKES 2 SERVINGS

8 cups lightly packed, tender lettuce, such as Boston,
   Bibb or red or green leaf, torn into bite-size pieces
1 medium tomato, cut into ½-inch dice
1 small carrot, peeled and shredded
1 (6⅛-ounce) can tuna in water or oil, drained and
   flaked
2 tablespoons olive oil
2 teaspoons red wine vinegar
⅛ teaspoon salt
Freshly ground black pepper
2 pita breads

1. In a medium bowl, toss together the lettuce, tomato, carrot and tuna. Drizzle the oil over the salad and toss again. Sprinkle on the vinegar, salt and pepper to taste; toss again.

2. Cut the pitas in half to make 4 pockets. With tongs, fill each pocket with about 2 cups of the tuna and salad mixture. Serve at once so the bread doesn't become soggy.

TUNA AND MARMALADE ON TOAST

▼▼▼▼▼

My cousin Alice swears by this lunchtime snack. It is, however, for marmalade lovers only.

MAKES 2 SERVINGS

4 slices of white bread

1½ tablespoons unsalted butter, softened

2 tablespoons orange marmalade

1 (6⅛-ounce) can solid white tuna in oil, drained and
  flaked

Freshly ground black pepper

Toast the bread slices and butter lightly while still warm. Top each slice with about 1½ teaspoons of marmalade. Divide the tuna fish on top and finish with several grindings of pepper. Cut in half and serve.

LIGHT TUNA SALAD
WITH LEMON
AND RELISH
▼▼▼▼▼

My colleague Malachy Duffy likes this tuna salad best on deli rye with lettuce. This recipe will give you enough salad for 2 to 3 sandwiches or stuffed tomatoes.

MAKES ABOUT 1⅔ CUPS

2 (6⅛-ounce) cans solid white tuna in water, drained
   and flaked
2 tablespoons reduced-fat mayonnaise
1 tablespoon fresh lemon juice
2 tablespoons hamburger relish or any sweet pickle
   relish
2 tablespoons minced onion
½ teaspoon freshly ground black pepper

Combine all the ingredients in a medium bowl. Mix with a fork until blended.

TUNA CLUB #1

▼▼▼▼▼

Although any of the tuna salad sandwich mixtures can be used here, I prefer the basic quality of Naked Tuna. Don't forget the toothpicks and potato chips!

MAKES 2 SANDWICHES

6 slices of lean bacon
6 slices of firm-textured white bread
About ¼ cup mayonnaise
1 recipe Naked Tuna Salad (page 44)
4 large ripe tomato slices, about ¼ inch thick
4 large lettuce leaves, such as romaine, Boston or
   iceberg, torn into large pieces

▼ THE TUNA FISH GOURMET ▼

1. Cook the bacon strips in a large heavy skillet over moderate heat, turning occasionally, until browned and crisp, about 5 minutes. Remove to paper towels to drain.

2. Toast the bread as desired. Lay 2 slices of toast on a flat work surface. Spread with mayonnaise. Divide the tuna salad mixture between the 2 slices, spreading evenly over the surface of the toast. Arrange 3 strips of the cooked bacon on top of each.

3. Spread a little more mayonnaise on 2 more slices of the toast and place a slice, mayonnaise-side down, on each serving of bacon. Spread a little more mayonnaise on top of the 2 slices and divide the tomato slices and lettuce over the tops.

4. Spread more mayonnaise on the remaining 2 slices of toast and invert one toast onto either sandwich. Insert 4 toothpicks into each sandwich and cut into quarters. Serve with potato chips and pickles.

TUNA CLUB #2

▼▼▼▼▼

To make junior clubs, just omit the middle slice of bread in each sandwich. I am partial to Herbed Tuna Salad in this sandwich. Vegetable slaw or potato salad are great accompaniments here.

MAKES 2 SANDWICHES

6 slices of whole wheat or whole-grain bread

2 tablespoons mayonnaise

2 teaspoons Dijon or grainy mustard

Herbed Tuna Salad (page 45)

2 hard-cooked eggs, sliced

4 large slices of ripe tomato, about ¼ inch thick

About ½ bunch watercress or arugula, tough stems
  removed

1. Lay the bread slices on a work surface. In a small bowl, stir together the mayonnaise and mustard until blended. Spread all but about 2 teaspoons of the mixture evenly over all the bread slices.

2. Spread the tuna salad over 2 of the bread slices. Arrange 1 of the sliced eggs over each, and cover each with another slice of bread, mustard mayonnaise-side down. Spread 1 teaspoon of the remaining mayonnaise mixture over each.

3. Arrange the tomato slices and the greens on top. Close with the remaining slices of bread. Cut the sandwiches in half and serve with a side of slaw or potato salad.

▼ THE TUNA FISH GOURMET ▼

CLASSIC TUNA MELT
▼▼▼▼▼

I took an informal poll among my friends, and although there are two schools of thought, the open-faced variety won out over the closed. While both styles are represented in this chapter, the recipe below represents the most classic melt, especially if made on an English muffin.

MAKES 4 OPEN-FACED MELTS, 2 SERVINGS

1 (6⅛-ounce) can solid white tuna in oil, drained and
   flaked
¼ cup minced celery
1 tablespoon minced onion
2½ tablespoons mayonnaise
Freshly ground black pepper
2 English muffins, split, or 4 slices of white bread
1 tablespoon unsalted butter, softened (optional)
8 slices of yellow American cheese

1. In a small bowl, stir together the tuna, celery, onion and mayonnaise with a fork until well blended. Season with pepper to taste and set aside.

2. Preheat the broiler. Toast the muffin halves or bread until golden. Lightly butter, if desired. Divide the tuna mixture among the 4 toasts, spreading evenly to cover.

3. Top each sandwich with 2 slices of cheese and broil for 1 to 2 minutes, until the cheese is melted.

PITA PIZZA-TUNA MELT

▼▼▼▼▼

As an hors d'oeuvre or a lunch treat, cut these pita melts into quarters for easy eating. Use fresh mozzarella, if available, and the best tomatoes you can find.

MAKES 4 SERVINGS

4 (6-inch) pita breads
4 teaspoons olive oil
1 (6⅛-ounce) can solid white tuna in oil, drained and
    lightly flaked
8 ounces mozzarella cheese, preferably lightly salted
    fresh
1 large ripe tomato (about ½ pound), quartered and
    seeded
4 teaspoons finely chopped fresh basil or 1 teaspoon
    dried
Freshly ground black pepper

1. Preheat the oven to 450°. Place the pita breads on a large baking sheet. Drizzle ½ teaspoon of the oil over each pita, then cover each with one-fourth of the tuna.

2. Slice the cheese as thinly as possible and divide among the breads, evenly covering the surface. Slice each of the tomato quarters crosswise and arrange the pieces over the cheese. Sprinkle ½ teaspoon of the remaining oil and 1 teaspoon of the fresh basil or ¼ teaspoon of the dried on top of each serving. Season with pepper to taste.

3. Bake for about 10 minutes, until the cheese is melted and bubbly and the edges are crispy brown. Let cool for several minutes before serving.

▼ THE TUNA FISH GOURMET ▼

SAN DIEGO MELT
WITH AVOCADO
ON TORTILLAS

▼▼▼▼▼

MAKES 2 SANDWICHES

2 (10-inch) flour tortillas
4 thin slices of pepper-jack cheese
1 recipe Confetti Tuna Salad (page 46)
¼ cup chopped ripe tomato
½ avocado, preferably Hass, pitted, peeled and cut
    lengthwise into ¼-inch-thick slices
Alfalfa sprouts (optional)

1. Preheat the broiler. Heat a large flameproof skillet over moderately high heat until hot, about 2 minutes. Place one of the tortillas in the pan. Place 2 slices of the cheese down the center of the tortilla and transfer to the broiler. Broil about 4 inches from the heat for 1 to 2 minutes, until melted. Remove to a plate and tent with foil to keep warm. Repeat with the remaining tortilla and cheese.

2. Transfer the tortillas to plates. Mound the tuna salad over the melted cheese on each tortilla, dividing evenly. Sprinkle the chopped tomato over the tuna and arrange about half the avocado slices diagonally down the center of each. Top with sprouts, if desired. Roll up like a burrito and serve at once.

TUNA MELT
WITH BACON AND
SWISS CHEESE
▼▼▼▼▼

This hearty melt is my husband Bob's favorite. We both enjoy it with crispy corn chips on the side.

MAKES 4 SANDWICHES

8 slices of pumpernickel or marbled pumpernickel-rye
   bread
2 to 3 tablespoons Thousand Island dressing
8 thin slices of imported Swiss cheese
8 slices of bacon, cooked until crisp*
1 recipe Naked Tuna Salad (page 44)
4 slices of large ripe tomato, cut about ¼ inch thick
2 to 3 tablespoons unsalted butter, softened

1. Arrange the bread in pairs on a flat work surface. Spread the salad dressing over all of the slices. Top each piece of bread with a slice of cheese, folding the cheese in half to fit if necessary.

2. Place 2 bacon slices on 4 of the slices and the tomato on the opposite 4. Spread the tuna on top of the 4 servings of bacon, then take the opposite halves of the sandwiches with the tomato slices and gently invert them on top of the tuna halves.

3. Preheat a large cast-iron or other heavy skillet or a griddle over moderate heat. Lightly spread the softened butter over both sides of each sandwich. Place the sandwiches in the preheated pan and cook until lightly toasted on the bottom, about 3 minutes. Carefully flip with a spatula and cook about 3 minutes longer, until the cheese is melted. Cut in half and serve immediately.

* To cook bacon, see page 55.

TUNA "CROQUE"
▼▼▼▼▼

The "Croque Monsieur" is France's most famous version of the grilled cheese sandwich. It is made with Swiss cheese and ham and usually a touch of mayonnaise. You can buy one in various bars, where one might stop for a coffee and a quick bite or from one of many food stands in Paris. My version uses tuna in place of the ham.

MAKES 2 SANDWICHES

1 (6⅛-ounce) can solid white tuna in water, drained
   and flaked
3½ tablespoons mayonnaise
¼ teaspoon freshly ground black pepper
4 slices of white bread
¾ cup shredded imported Swiss cheese, such as
   Gruyère, Emmenthaler, Finlandia or Jarlsberg (about
   3 ounces)
2 tablespoons unsalted butter, softened

1. In a medium bowl, combine the tuna with 2 tablespoons of the mayonnaise and the pepper. Cover and refrigerate until ready to use.

2. Lightly spread the remaining mayonnaise over one side of each of the 4 bread slices. Divide the cheese among all 4 slices, distributing it evenly. Spoon half of the tuna mixture onto 2 of the slices over the cheese and cover with the remaining 2 slices of cheese-covered bread, mayonnaise-side down.

3. Place a heavy medium skillet, preferably cast-iron, over moderately low heat for about 2 minutes to heat up. Spread the softened butter on the top and bottom of both sandwiches and place the sandwiches in the hot pan. Cook until nicely browned on the bottom, about 2 minutes. Flip and cook until browned on the other side, about 2 minutes longer. The cheese should be melted but not runny.

4. With a wide spatula, transfer the sandwiches to a cutting board. Cut in half and serve at once.

▼ THE TUNA FISH GOURMET ▼

BAGEL MELT

▼▼▼▼▼

Fresh bagels—slightly crisp on the outside and chewy on the inside—are a must for this perfect luncheon fare.

MAKES 4 OPEN-FACE HALVES

2 fresh bagels of any savory flavor
2 tablespoons mayonnaise
4 paper-thin slices of onion, preferably Walla Walla,
   Vidalia or other sweet variety
1 recipe Naked Tuna Salad (page 44)
4 (4-by-4-inch) slices of Havarti cheese

1. Preheat the broiler. Split the bagels horizontally and divide the mayonnaise among the 4 halves, spreading evenly. Place an onion slice on top of each. Mound a generous ⅓ cup of the tuna salad over the onion on each bagel half.

2. Top with the cheese and broil 3 to 4 inches from the heat for 1 to 2 minutes, until melted.

SEMOLINA MELT

▼▼▼▼▼

MAKES A 12-INCH SUBMARINE MELT, TO SERVE 2

1 (12-inch) loaf of semolina bread, split horizontally in
   half
1 recipe Tuna Salad Siciliano (page 47)
1½ tablespoons capers, rinsed and drained
¾ cup shredded Italian Fontina cheese (about 3 ounces)

1. Preheat the broiler. Place the semolina halves under the broiler about 6
inches from the heat and toast lightly, 2 to 3 minutes. Set the top of the loaf
aside.

2. Make the tuna salad and spread it over the bottom half of bread. Sprinkle
the capers over the tuna. Distribute the cheese evenly on top.

3. Broil about 4 inches from the heat for 1 to 2 minutes, until the cheese is
melted. Cover with the reserved top half, cut the submarine crosswise into 4
pieces and serve immediately.

CHAPTER 4
▼▼▼▼▼
IN THE SALAD BOWL

TOMATOES STUFFED WITH TUNA SALAD

HEALTH SALAD WITH TUNA

SPINACH AND TUNA SALAD WITH EASY ORANGE VINAIGRETTE

TUNA TABBOULEH

TUNA AND BROWN RICE SALAD WITH CARROTS, RAISINS AND TOFU

TUNA AND WATERCRESS SALAD

TUNA SALAD NIÇOISE

TUNA AND BROCCOLI WITH CHERRY TOMATOES, SCALLIONS AND CAPERS

CURRIED TUNA WITH WILD RICE SALAD

TUNA COBB SALAD

COOL RED CABBAGE WITH TUNA AND FENNEL

SALAD OF TUNA, LENTILS AND ARUGULA

WARM SALAD OF TUNA AND CANNELLINI BEANS

TWO BEAN AND TUNA SALAD

TRACEY'S FAVORITE SALAD WITH TUNA

TUNA AND PASTA SALAD

NEW POTATO AND TUNA SALAD WITH BASIL AND OIL

TOMATOES STUFFED
WITH TUNA SALAD
▼▼▼▼▼

A late summertime favorite, when delicious, red ripe tomatoes are in abundance. I like to serve Melba toasts on the side to add some crunch.

MAKES 2 SERVINGS

1 (6⅛-ounce) can solid white tuna in water or oil,
   drained and flaked

1 large celery rib, halved lengthwise and thinly sliced
   crosswise

2 tablespoons finely chopped green bell pepper

1 tablespoon finely chopped red onion

¼ teaspoon freshly ground black pepper

2 teaspoons fresh lemon juice

2 to 3 tablespoons mayonnaise

6 to 8 large lettuce leaves

2 medium-size ripe tomatoes

¼ cup grated yellow Cheddar cheese (optional)

1. In a medium bowl, toss together the tuna, celery, bell pepper, red onion and black pepper. Add the lemon juice and mayonnaise and stir with a fork until blended. (If desired, cover and refrigerate overnight.)

2. Arrange several lettuce leaves on 2 individual plates. With a small, sharp knife, remove the core from 1 of the tomatoes. Then, slice through the tomato, starting at the top and stopping about ¼ inch from the bottom. Rotate the fruit and slice through 2 more times so that there are 6 even wedges cut that are still attached in the center at the bottom. Repeat with the remaining tomato.

3. Place a prepared tomato on each of the 2 beds of lettuce. Spoon half of the tuna mixture into each tomato. Sprinkle each with half the cheese, if desired.

HEALTH SALAD
WITH TUNA
▼▼▼▼▼

Almost any raw vegetable in season can be dried and added to this low-calorie toss. Serve it as a side dish or as a main course over chilled pasta, rice or greens. The salad keeps for several days in the refrigerator.

MAKES 4 TO 6 SERVINGS

1 small green bell pepper, cut into ¼-inch dice (⅔ cup)

1 small red bell pepper, cut into ¼-inch dice (⅔ cup)

3 small zucchini, cut into ¼-inch dice (1⅓ cups)

2 small yellow squash, cut into ¼-inch dice (⅔ cup)

3 medium carrots, peeled and grated

1 medium cucumber, peeled, quartered lengthwise,
    seeded and cut into ¼-inch dice (1¼ cups)

2 tablespoons mild olive oil

2 tablespoons red wine vinegar

½ to ¾ teaspoon salt, to taste

½ teaspoon freshly ground black pepper

2 (6⅛-ounce) cans solid white tuna in water, drained
   and flaked
2 medium tomatoes, seeded and cut into ⅜-inch dice
¼ cup finely chopped fresh parsley

1. In a large bowl, toss together the green pepper, red pepper, zucchini, yellow squash, carrots and cucumber.

2. Drizzle the oil over the vegetables and toss to coat. Sprinkle on the vinegar and season with the salt and pepper. Toss again. (The recipe can be made to this point 1 day ahead, cover and refrigerate overnight.)

3. Add the tuna, tomatoes and parsley to the salad and toss. Taste and adjust the seasoning if necessary.

▼ THE TUNA FISH GOURMET ▼

SPINACH AND TUNA SALAD WITH EASY ORANGE VINAIGRETTE

▼▼▼▼▼

In this light, refreshing and satisfying salad, the heat of red onion is cooled by a short marination in red wine vinegar and fresh orange juice.

MAKES 4 MAIN-COURSE SERVINGS

1 medium red onion, peeled, halved and thinly sliced

2 tablespoons red wine vinegar

2 medium navel oranges

2 (12-ounce) bunches of spinach, preferably tender flat-leaf spinach, stemmed, rinsed and dried (about 8 cups)

1 medium Belgian endive, thinly sliced crosswise

⅓ cup matchstick slices of jicama or water chestnuts

1 (6⅛-ounce) can solid white tuna in water, drained and flaked

1 teaspoon Dijon mustard

½ cup olive oil

¼ teaspoon salt

¼ teaspoon freshly ground black pepper

1. Place the red onion slices in a small bowl, toss with the vinegar and set aside. Grate the skin of 1 of the oranges on the fine holes of a box grater, avoiding the bitter white pith, to obtain 1 teaspoon of the colored zest. Place in a separate small bowl. Cut this orange in half and squeeze out the juice. Pour the juice over the onion.

2. With a small sharp knife, cut the peel off the other orange, removing all the bitter pith. Carefully cut in along both sides of the lines of membrane to release the orange sections and reserve.

3. Mound the spinach on 4 larger plates. Distribute the endive, jicama, tuna and reserved orange sections over the spinach. Drain the onion, pouring the liquid into the bowl with the orange zest. Scatter the onion slices on top of the salads.

4. Whisk the mustard into the orange juice mixture until blended. Gradually whisk in the oil, pouring in a fine stream until incorporated. Season with the salt and pepper. Serve the salads immediately, with the dressing passed on the side.

TUNA TABBOULEH
▼▼▼▼▼

This light and satisfying main-dish salad contains the whole-grain goodness of bulghur, or cracked wheat.

MAKES 4 SERVINGS

1 cup bulghur wheat

⅓ cup olive oil

2 medium tomatoes, cut into ¼-inch dice

2 (6⅛-ounce) cans solid white tuna in water, drained
   and flaked

3 medium scallions, thinly sliced

2 tablespoons fresh lemon juice

⅓ cup chopped fresh cilantro

½ teaspoon salt

¾ teaspoon freshly ground black pepper

1. Bring 3 cups of water to a boil in a medium saucepan over moderately high heat. Stir in the bulghur. Reduce the heat to low, cover and let simmer for 15 to 20 minutes, until the bulghur is tender. Drain into a sieve to remove the excess water. Let the bulghur cool to room temperature, about 15 minutes.

2. Place the cooled bulghur in a bowl. Add the olive oil and stir to combine. Add the tomatoes, tuna, scallions, lemon juice, cilantro, salt and pepper. Toss to blend. Serve immediately or cover and refrigerate for several hours before serving.

▼ THE TUNA FISH GOURMET ▼

TUNA AND BROWN RICE SALAD WITH CARROTS, RAISINS AND TOFU

▼▼▼▼▼

Cubes of tofu give this salad an extra boost of protein. Serve with hearty slices of whole-grain bread.

MAKES 2 TO 3 SERVINGS

1 teaspoon salt

½ cup uncooked brown rice

1 (6⅛-ounce) can solid white tuna in water, drained
   and lightly flaked

2 medium carrots, peeled and shredded

2 tablespoons raisins

1 medium celery rib, thinly sliced

1 (3- to 4-ounce) block of medium-firm tofu, cut into
   ½-inch cubes

1 teaspoon grainy mustard

1 tablespoon white wine vinegar

2 tablespoons finely chopped fresh herbs, such as
    marjoram, basil, thyme and/or chives
½ teaspoon pepper
3 tablespoons safflower or other light vegetable oil

1. In a small saucepan over moderately high heat, bring 1¼ cups of water and
½ teaspoon of the salt to a boil. Stir in the rice, cover and reduce the heat to
low. Continue cooking until the rice is tender and most of the water has been
absorbed, about 45 minutes. Drain if necessary.

2. In a large bowl, toss together the brown rice, tuna, carrots, raisins, celery
and tofu.

3. In a small bowl, whisk together the mustard, vinegar, herbs, remaining ½
teaspoon salt and the pepper. Gradually whisk in the oil until blended. Toss
the dressing with the tuna and rice mixture and serve.

TUNA AND WATERCRESS SALAD

▼▼▼▼▼

Plenty of greens, including the slight bitterness of endive and sharpness of watercress, ensures a salad that is refreshing and light.

MAKES 6 SERVINGS

1 medium head of romaine lettuce

3 (6½-ounce) cans tuna in olive oil, drained and flaked

2 bunches of watercress, large stems removed

1 large Belgian endive, thinly sliced crosswise

¼ cup chopped red onion

3 tablespoons olive oil

2 teaspoons fresh lemon juice

½ teaspoon freshly ground black pepper

¼ teaspoon salt

1. Using a large sharp knife and starting at the green, leafy end of the head, very thinly slice the romaine crosswise to make shreds. Rinse and dry. Place on a platter or individual serving plates.

2. In a large bowl, toss together the tuna, watercress, endive and red onion. Drizzle on the olive oil and toss again to coat; then toss with the lemon juice. Add the pepper and salt and toss again. Mound the tuna and watercress mixture on top of the bed(s) of romaine. Serve immediately.

TUNA SALAD NICOISE
▼▼▼▼▼

No main-course salad is more classic than this one. Thin French beans, called haricots verts, *are especially nice in this recipe if you can find them at your local market.*

MAKES 4 MAIN-DISH OR 8 FIRST-COURSE SERVINGS

½ pound small red potatoes, scrubbed

6 large eggs

6 ounces green beans, ends trimmed

¼ cup Dijon mustard

¼ cup red wine vinegar

¼ teaspoon freshly ground black pepper

½ cup mild olive oil

8 cups lightly packed torn pieces of romaine lettuce
    (about 12 ounces), rinsed and dried

2 (6½-ounce) cans tuna in olive oil, drained and flaked

4 small tomatoes, cut into wedges

8 anchovy fillets, rinsed and patted dry (optional)

½ cup Niçoise or other oil-cured black olives, for
    garnish

1. Place the potatoes in a medium saucepan and add lightly salted water to cover. Bring to a boil over moderately high heat. Reduce the heat slightly and boil until tender, about 15 minutes, depending on the size. Drain and let cool. Do not rinse.

2. Meanwhile, place the eggs in a medium saucepan and add water to cover. Bring to a boil over moderate heat. Boil gently for 10 minutes. Drain and rinse in several changes of cold water until cool. Peel the eggs and set aside.

3. Bring a medium saucepan with 2 inches of water to a boil over moderately high heat. Add the green beans and cook until just tender, about 5 minutes. Drain and rinse under cold running water; drain well.

4. In a small bowl, whisk together the mustard, vinegar and pepper. Gradually whisk in the oil in a thin stream until well blended. Set the dressing aside.

5. Arrange the lettuce on a platter. Place a mound of tuna in the center. Arrange the green beans around the tuna. Quarter the hard-cooked eggs and potatoes and distribute them and the tomato wedges over the top of the lettuce and around the edge of the salad. Garnish with the anchovies and olives. Pass the dressing on the side.

TUNA AND BROCCOLI WITH CHERRY TOMATOES, SCALLIONS AND CAPERS

▼▼▼▼▼

MAKES 4 SERVINGS

1 bunch of broccoli (about 1¼ pounds), cut into
   ½-inch florets
1 pint cherry tomatoes, halved
1 (6½-ounce) can tuna in olive oil, drained and lightly
   flaked
1 anchovy fillet, rinsed and mashed, or 1 teaspoon
   anchovy paste
1 small garlic clove, crushed through a press
1½ teaspoons fresh lemon juice
1 teaspoon Dijon mustard
1½ tablespoons red wine vinegar
3 tablespoons olive oil
½ teaspoon freshly ground black pepper

Salt (optional)

2 scallions, thinly sliced

¼ cup capers, rinsed and drained

1. Insert a steamer in a large saucepan with 1 inch of water and place over moderately high heat. Arrange the broccoli florets in the steamer, cover with a lid and cook for about 7 minutes, or until just tender. Drain, rinse under cold water to cool and drain well. Place the broccoli in a large bowl with the cherry tomatoes and tuna and toss to combine. Set aside.

2. In a small bowl, whisk together the mashed anchovy, garlic, lemon juice mustard and vinegar until blended. Gradually whisk in the olive oil until well blended. Season with the pepper and salt to taste. Stir in the scallions and capers.

3. Pour the dressing over the broccoli and tuna salad and toss to coat. Serve immediately or let stand for up to 3 hours to let the flavors blend.

CURRIED TUNA WITH WILD RICE SALAD

▼▼▼▼▼

A hint of curry combined with the tartness of lemon juice and sweetness of grapes makes this an especially appealing salad. If you happen to have leftover cooked wild rice, you will need about 2 cups of it to make this recipe.

MAKES 4 SERVINGS

½ cup uncooked wild rice

2 (6⅛-ounce) cans solid white tuna in water, drained
   and lightly flaked

1 large celery rib, thinly sliced

½ cup diced, peeled and seeded cucumber

1 cup seedless red grapes, halved

⅓ cup mayonnaise

¼ cup sour cream

1½ tablespoons fresh lemon juice

¼ teaspoon Madras (hot) curry powder

¼ teaspoon salt

¼ teaspoon freshly ground black pepper
Large leaves of Boston lettuce, for serving
Cucumber slices, for garnish

1. Place the wild rice and 2 cups of lightly salted water in a small saucepan over moderately high heat. Bring to a boil, reduce the heat to low, cover the pan and simmer until the rice is popped open and tender, about 40 minutes. Drain and let cool.

2. When the rice is cool, transfer to a large bowl. Add the tuna, celery, cucumber and grapes. Toss to mix.

3. In a small bowl, whisk together the mayonnaise, sour cream, lemon juice, curry powder, salt and pepper. Scrape the dressing over the tuna-wild rice salad and stir to blend.

4. Arrange leaves of Boston lettuce on 4 individual plates. Spoon about 1½ cups of the salad onto each bed of lettuce and serve, garnished with cucumber slices.

▼ THE TUNA FISH GOURMET ▼

TUNA COBB SALAD

▼▼▼▼▼

Tuna makes a fine alternative to the classic chicken in this attractive composed salad. It can be served with any dressing of choice; creamy blue cheese, Thousand Island and creamy garlic are especially delicious with the combination of flavors here.

MAKES 4 SERVINGS

4 large eggs

½ pound lean bacon

1 head of romaine lettuce, torn into bite-size pieces
   (about 8 cups), well chilled

1 large tomato, cut into ⅜-inch dice

2 ripe avocados, preferably Hass, halved, seeded,
   peeled and diced

2 (6⅛-ounce) cans solid white tuna in water, drained
   and flaked

⅓ cup coarsely chopped black olives

1. Place the eggs in a medium saucepan with water to cover. Bring to a boil over moderately high heat, reduce the heat to moderate and boil gently for 10 minutes. Drain and rinse with several changes of cold water until the eggs have cooled. Peel and reserve.

2. Meanwhile, in a large skillet, cook the bacon over moderate heat until crisp, about 6 minutes. Drain on paper towels, crumble and set aside.

3. Place the lettuce in the bottom of a large serving bowl. Arrange the tomato pieces down the center of the lettuce to make a red stripe. Make a line of avocado to one side of the tomato and a line of tuna on the other. Continue with the olives next to the avocado. Chop the eggs and arrange them in a line next to the tuna. Sprinkle the bacon over all. Serve immediately with a dressing of your choice or simply cruets of olive oil and vinegar on the side.

COOL RED CABBAGE WITH TUNA AND FENNEL

▼▼▼▼▼

Crisp, colorful and cool, this delightful first-course salad can be doubled or tripled easily to serve as part of an antipasto plate or to add to a buffet table. You can prepare the cabbage and fennel up to three days ahead, but toss in the tuna and olives just before serving.

MAKES 4 FIRST-COURSE SERVINGS

1 medium bulb of fennel, quartered and shredded

¼ small (1-pound) red cabbage, shredded or very thinly
   sliced

1 medium onion, thinly sliced

2 tablespoons rice wine vinegar

2 teaspoons Dijon mustard

2 tablespoons olive oil

¼ teaspoon salt

½ teaspoon freshly ground black pepper

1 (6½-ounce) can tuna in olive oil, drained and flaked

2 tablespoons minced fresh parsley

½ cup pitted Calamata or other oil-cured black olives,
coarsely chopped

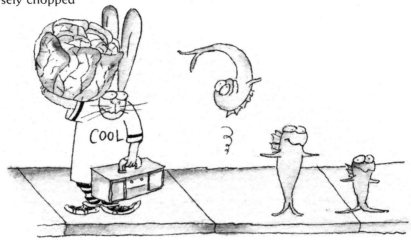

1. In a medium bowl, combine the fennel, cabbage and onion. Toss to mix.

2. In a small bowl, whisk together the vinegar, mustard, oil, salt and pepper until blended. Pour over the cabbage mixture and toss to coat. (The recipe can be prepared to this point up to 3 days ahead; cover and refrigerate.)

3. Add the tuna, parsley and olives to the cabbage mixture. Toss to mix. Serve immediately.

▼ THE TUNA FISH GOURMET ▼

SALAD OF TUNA, LENTILS AND ARUGULA

▼▼▼▼▼

You can make this salad with brown, red or tiny French green lentils; just adjust the cooking time according to the package directions.

MAKES 4 TO 6 SERVINGS

1 cup brown lentils (7 ounces)

2 teaspoons minced fresh thyme or ½ teaspoon dried

¾ teaspoon salt

¾ teaspoon freshly ground black pepper

2 (6½-ounce) cans tuna in olive oil, drained and flaked

2 medium scallions, thinly sliced

5 tablespoons extra-virgin olive oil

1 tablespoon plus 1 teaspoon balsamic vinegar

1 bunch of arugula, large stems removed

1 teaspoon fresh lemon juice

1. Place the lentils in a medium saucepan and add 3 cups of water. Bring to a boil over moderately high heat, reduce the heat to moderate and boil gently until the lentils are tender, about 25 minutes. Do not overcook. Drain and rinse with cold water until cool; drain well.

2. In a large bowl, combine the lentils with the thyme and ½ teaspoon each of salt and pepper. Stir in the tuna, scallions, 3 tablespoons of the olive oil and the vinegar.

3. In a medium bowl, toss the arugula with the remaining 2 tablespoons olive oil to coat. Sprinkle on the lemon juice and the remaining ¼ teaspoon each salt and pepper. Toss to mix.

4. Divide the lentil and tuna mixture among 4 or 6 plates. Surround with the arugula.

WARM SALAD OF TUNA AND CANNELLINI BEANS
▼▼▼▼▼

There are many versions of this Tuscan dish, which is usually served as part of an antipasto or as a first course. I like it as a side dish or as an appetizer with garlic toasts (page 7).

MAKES 8 SERVINGS

2 cups dried cannellini beans, rinsed, picked over and
    soaked overnight (see Note, below)

½ teaspoon salt

2 tablespoons extra-virgin olive oil

1 small onion, finely chopped

2 medium garlic cloves, minced

1 tablespoon finely chopped fresh sage or ½ teaspoon
    dried

2 teaspoons Dijon mustard

2 tablespoons red wine vinegar

⅓ cup mayonnaise

2 (6½-ounce) cans tuna, preferably in olive oil, drained
  and flaked
2 tablespoons finely chopped fresh parsley
Freshly ground black pepper

1. Place the beans in a medium saucepan with cold water to cover by 1 inch.
Bring to a boil over moderate heat and continue to cook for 3 minutes. Drain
and rinse the beans well, return to the saucepan and add water to cover by
2 inches. Bring to a boil over moderate heat. Reduce the heat to maintain a
simmer and cook for about 1 hour, until the beans are tender but not mushy.
Remove from the heat, stir in the salt and let stand while you make the
dressing.

2. Heat the oil in a small skillet over moderately low heat. Add the onion,
garlic and sage and cook until the onion is softened, about 4 minutes. Transfer
to a large bowl. Let cool. Whisk in the mustard, vinegar and mayonnaise.

3. Drain the warm beans and fold them into the mayonnaise mixture along
with the tuna and parsley. Stir in plenty of pepper and season with additional
salt to taste. Let stand for up to 3 hours before serving or serve immediately.

Note: If time doesn't permit overnight soaking of the beans, follow the
package directions for the quick-soak method.

TWO BEAN AND TUNA SALAD

▼▼▼▼▼

MAKES 4 TO 6 SERVINGS

½ pound fresh wax beans, stemmed

½ pound thin green beans, stemmed

Salt

⅓ cup olive oil

1 large garlic clove, very thinly sliced lengthwise

1 small red bell pepper, cut into 2-by-¼-inch strips

2 (6½-ounce) cans tuna in olive oil, drained and flaked

2 tablespoons chopped fresh basil or Italian parsley

½ teaspoon freshly ground black pepper

1. Bring 1 inch of lightly salted water to a boil in a medium saucepan over moderately high heat. Add the wax beans, cover and cook until just tender, about 8 minutes. Remove with a slotted spoon or tongs and set aside to cool. Place the green beans in the saucepan, cover and cook until tender, 5 to 6 minutes. Set aside with the wax beans.

2. Heat the olive oil in a large skillet over low heat. Add the garlic slices and cook, stirring until softened and fragrant, about 2 minutes; do not brown. Stir in the bell pepper strips and cook, until softened, about 4 minutes.

3. Add the cooked beans, increase the heat to moderate and cook, stirring, until well combined and hot. Stir in the tuna, basil and black pepper. Serve warm or at room temperature.

▼ THE TUNA FISH GOURMET ▼

TRACEY'S FAVORITE
SALAD WITH TUNA
▼▼▼▼▼

Here's a perfect luncheon salad that incorporates leftover cooked potatoes and greens. The oil and vinegar dressing is simple, light and takes no time to make.

MAKES 2 SERVINGS

1 medium garlic clove, halved

4 cups lettuce torn in bite-size pieces, such as romaine,
    Boston, red or green leaf

2 small tomatoes, cut into wedges

4 cooked small red potatoes, chilled and sliced

¼ cup thinly sliced scallion greens

1 (6⅛- or 6½-ounce) can of tuna in water or vegetable
    or olive oil, drained and flaked

1½ tablespoons extra-virgin or mild olive oil

2 teaspoons red wine vinegar

Salt and freshly ground pepper

1. Rub a large salad bowl, preferably a wooden one, with the cut garlic clove. In the bowl, toss together the lettuce, tomatoes, potato slices, scallion greens and tuna.

2. Drizzle the olive oil over the salad and toss to coat. Sprinkle on the vinegar, toss and season with salt and pepper to taste. Serve immediately.

▼ THE TUNA FISH GOURMET ▼

TUNA AND
PASTA SALAD
▼▼▼▼▼

For a simple balanced lunch, serve with a small lettuce and tomato salad.

MAKES ABOUT 6 CUPS, 4 SERVINGS

½ pound spiral pasta, such as fusilli

1 (6⅛-ounce) can solid white tuna in oil, drained

¼ cup finely chopped red onion

½ cup thinly sliced celery

¼ cup to 6 tablespoons mayonnaise

1 tablespoon distilled white or white wine vinegar

½ teaspoon freshly ground black pepper

1. Cook the pasta in a large pot of boiling salted water until *al dente*, tender but still slightly resistant to the bite, 10 to 12 minutes. Drain, rinse under cold running water to cool and drain well. In a large bowl, toss the pasta with the tuna, red onion and celery.

2. In a small bowl, whisk together ¼ cup of the mayonnaise, the vinegar and pepper. Stir the mayonnaise mixture into the pasta mixture. Add the remaining mayonnaise if necessary for moistness. Serve at room temperature, or cover and refrigerate until chilled for up to 2 days.

▼ THE TUNA FISH GOURMET ▼

NEW POTATO AND TUNA SALAD WITH BASIL AND OIL

▼▼▼▼▼

Serve this dish slightly warm or at room temperature.

MAKES 4 TO 6 SERVINGS

1½ pounds small red potatoes

¼ cup olive oil

2 tablespoons finely chopped fresh basil

1 (6⅛-ounce) can solid white tuna in oil, drained

¼ to ½ teaspoon freshly ground black pepper, to taste

⅛ teaspoon salt

1. Place the potatoes in a medium saucepan with lightly salted water to cover. Bring to a boil over moderately high heat. Reduce the heat slightly and boil until the potatoes are fork-tender, 12 to 15 minutes. Drain and let cool.

2. Cut the potatoes in halves or quarters and place in a large bowl. Pour on the olive oil and toss gently to coat. Add the basil, tuna, pepper and salt and toss again.

CHAPTER 5
▼▼▼▼▼
SATISFYING SUPPERS

TUNA NOODLE CASSEROLE

▼▼▼▼▼

Whether because of its nostalgic appeal, convenience or taste—or a combination of the three —this casserole has become an American classic.

MAKES 4 SERVINGS

2 cups medium elbow macaroni

1 (6⅛-ounce) can solid white tuna in oil, drained and
   flaked

1 cup fresh or thawed frozen peas

¾ cup finely chopped onion

1 (10½-ounce) can cream of mushroom soup

1 (10½-ounce) can cream of celery soup

⅓ cup milk or water

½ teaspoon black pepper, or more to taste

¼ pound saltine crackers (1 sleeve), crushed

1. Preheat the oven to 375°. Cook the macaroni in a large saucepan of boiling salted water, stirring occasionally, until just tender, 6 to 8 minutes. Drain and place in a large bowl. Add the tuna, peas and onion and toss to combine.

2. In a medium bowl, whisk together the mushroom and celery soups, milk and pepper. Pour over the macaroni mixture, scraping the sides of the bowl with a rubber spatula to include all the liquid, and toss to incorporate. Spoon the mixture evenly into a lightly buttered shallow 2-quart casserole. Sprinkle the crumbled saltines over the top.

3. Bake until the casserole is piping hot throughout and the top is golden, about 45 minutes. Let cool slightly before serving.

▼ THE TUNA FISH GOURMET ▼

TUNA DREAM DISH

▼▼▼▼▼

My friend Joy created this recipe for her boyfriend in college. They're still eating it after fifteen years of marriage.

MAKES 2 TO 3 SERVINGS

½ pound spaghetti, broken in half

1 egg, in the shell

2½ tablespoons unsalted butter

2 tablespoons all-purpose flour

1½ cups milk

4 ounces shredded mozzarella cheese (about 1 cup)

1 (6⅛-ounce) can solid white tuna in oil, drained and
    lightly flaked

Freshly ground black pepper

1 tablespoon minced fresh parsley

1. Bring a large pot of salted water to a boil over moderately high heat. Add the spaghetti and gently place the egg in the pot, taking care not to crack the shell. Cook the pasta, stirring gently occasionally, until *al dente*, tender but still slightly resistant to the bite, 8 to 10 minutes.

2. While the pasta is cooking, make the sauce. In a medium saucepan, melt 2 tablespoons of the butter over moderately high heat. Sprinkle in the flour and cook, stirring, for 1 minute. Gradually whisk in the milk and bring to a boil, stirring, until smooth and thickened, 2 to 3 minutes. Stir in the mozzarella and flaked tuna. Remove from the heat. Cover to keep warm.

3. Drain the pasta well. Set the egg aside to cool. Transfer the spaghetti to a large bowl and stir in the remaining ½ tablespoon butter. Pour the sauce over the pasta and toss to distribute well. Season generously with freshly ground pepper and toss again. Peel and slice the hard-cooked egg and arrange over the top. Garnish with the chopped parsley and serve immediately.

▼ THE TUNA FISH GOURMET ▼

LINGUINE WITH RED TUNA SAUCE
▼▼▼▼▼

A simple yet robust dish that can be ready in less than an hour. It is loaded with fresh herbs and is especially delicious made with vine-ripened summer plum tomatoes.

MAKES 2 SERVINGS

2 tablespoons extra-virgin olive oil

1 small onion, finely chopped

2 large garlic cloves, minced

1 (28-ounce) can Italian-style peeled tomatoes,
   coarsely chopped, with their liquid

1 tablespoon fresh rosemary leaves, chopped, or
   1 teaspoon dried, crumbled

1 teaspoon fresh thyme leaves or ½ teaspoon dried

½ pound linguine

1 (6⅛-ounce) can tuna in oil, drained and lightly flaked

2 tablespoons minced chives

¼ teaspoon salt
½ teaspoon freshly ground black pepper
Parmesan cheese, as accompaniment

1. In a large nonreactive skillet, warm the oil over moderately low heat. Add the onion and garlic and cook, stirring occasionally, until softened but not browned, 5 to 6 minutes. Add the tomatoes with their liquid, the rosemary and the thyme. Partially cover and cook, stirring occasionally, until thickened, about 30 minutes.

2. Meanwhile, bring a large saucepan of salted water to a boil over moderately high heat. Add the linguine and cook, stirring often, until *al dente*, tender but still slightly resistant to the bite, 8 to 10 minutes. Drain well, return the pasta to the pot and set aside in a warm spot.

3. To the tomato sauce, add the tuna, chives, salt and pepper. Stir over moderate heat until heated through, about 1 minute. Scrape the sauce over the linguine and toss to combine. Serve immediately with a bowl of grated Parmesan cheese on the side.

SPAGHETTINI WITH TUNA, SPINACH AND SAUSAGE

▼▼▼▼▼

MAKES 2 SERVINGS

4 ounces sausage links (2 to 4 sausages, Italian or
   breakfast)

1 (12-ounce) bunch of tender spinach leaves, stemmed
   and soaked

¼ cup mild olive oil

2 large garlic cloves, very thinly sliced

¼ teaspoon salt

¼ teaspoon freshly ground black pepper

½ pound spaghettini (thin spaghetti)

1 (6½-ounce) can tuna in olive oil, drained

1. Cook the sausage in a large nonreactive skillet over moderately high heat, turning, until nicely browned and no longer pink in the center, about 10 minutes. Remove to paper towels to drain. Cut the sausage into bite-size pieces. Pour off the fat from the skillet.

2. Add the spinach to the skillet and cook over moderately high heat, stirring, until wilted, 1 to 2 minutes. Scrape the contents of the pan onto a plate. Roughly cut up the spinach with a knife and fork and reserve.

3. Heat the olive oil in the same skillet. Add the garlic and cook over low heat, stirring, for 1 minute. Do not brown. Add the spinach and sausage and season with the salt and pepper. Remove from the heat and set aside.

4. Cook the spaghettini in a large pot of salted water until *al dente,* tender but still slightly resistant to the bite, 6 to 8 minutes. Drain, but do not rinse. Heat the spinach and sausage mixture over moderately high heat until hot, about 1 minute. Add the tuna and break it up slightly. Add the spaghettini and toss to mix. Serve at once.

QUICK TUNA
NOODLE DELIGHT
▼▼▼▼▼

Fresh summer basil is what makes this quick dish so special. In authentic Italian fashion, some of the pasta cooking liquid is incorporated into the sauce.

MAKES 4 SERVINGS

1 pound spaghettini (thin spaghetti)

⅔ cup mild olive oil

2 large garlic cloves, finely chopped

2 (6⅛-ounce) cans tuna in oil, drained and lightly
   flaked

2 medium tomatoes, cut into ½-inch dice (optional)

½ cup chopped fresh basil

½ teaspoon freshly ground black pepper

¼ teaspoon salt

1. Bring a large pot of salted water to a boil over moderately high heat. Add the spaghettini and cook until *al dente*, tender but still slightly resistant to the bite, 6 to 8 minutes.

2. While the pasta is cooking, make the sauce. Heat the olive oil in a large skillet over moderately low heat. Add the garlic and cook, stirring, until softened but not browned, about 2 minutes. Ladle in ⅔ cup of the pasta cooking water. Remove the sauce from the heat until the pasta is cooked.

3. Drain the spaghettini. Place the skillet with the sauce over moderately high heat and bring to a boil. Stir in the tuna, tomatoes (if using), the basil, pepper and salt. Add the pasta to the skillet and toss to combine. Serve warm.

SEAMAN'S PIE

▼▼▼▼▼

This combination of tuna and garlicky mashed potatoes makes everyone ask for seconds!

MAKES 4 TO 6 SERVINGS

6 tablespoons unsalted butter

¼ cup all-purpose flour

2½ cups milk

½ teaspoon freshly ground black pepper

2 cups fresh peas (from 2 pounds pea pods), or

    1 (10-ounce) package frozen peas

4 large baking potatoes, preferably Idaho, peeled and

    cut into 1-inch chunks

3 garlic cloves, halved

¾ teaspoon salt

2 (6⅛-ounce) cans solid white tuna in oil, drained

1. In a medium saucepan, melt 2 tablespoons of the butter over moderate heat. Stir in the flour to form a paste and continue to cook, stirring, for 2 minutes without allowing the flour to color. Gradually whisk in 2 cups of the milk, ½ cup at a time. Bring to a boil, whisking until smooth and thickened, about 2 minutes. Reduce the heat to moderately low and simmer 3 minutes longer. Remove from the heat. Stir in ¼ teaspoon pepper. Scrape the white sauce into a 9-inch round soufflé dish or deep casserole. Set aside to cool.

2. Bring a small saucepan with 2 inches of water to a boil over moderately high heat. Add the fresh or frozen peas and boil for 2 minutes. Drain and rinse under cold running water; drain well.

3. Preheat the oven to 350°. Place the potatoes and garlic in a large saucepan with water to cover and ¼ teaspoon of the salt. Bring to a boil over moderately high heat, reduce the heat slightly and boil gently until tender, about 12 minutes; drain. Mash the potatoes by pressing them through a food mill or ricer into a large bowl. With a wooden spoon, beat in the remaining 4 tablespoons butter, ½ teaspoon salt and ¼ teaspoon pepper. Gradually beat in the remaining ½ cup milk.

4. Stir the tuna into the cooled white sauce. Spoon the peas over the top in an even layer. Evenly mound the mashed potatoes on top, covering the whole surface. Bake in the hot oven 40 to 45 minutes, until the tips of the potatoes are golden brown.

PANTRY RIGATONI

▼▼▼▼▼

A boon for after-work cooks, this healthy dish utilizes many ingredients that can be stored on the shelf for last-minute company.

MAKES 2 TO 4 SERVINGS

1 tablespoon olive oil

¼ pound fresh mushrooms, sliced

½ medium onion, finely chopped

2 large garlic cloves, thinly sliced

1 cup canned reduced-sodium chicken broth

½ pound rigatoni

3 marinated artichoke hearts, quartered

1 (6⅛-ounce) can solid white tuna in oil, drained and
   flaked

8 sun-dried, oil-packed tomato halves, cut in ¼-inch
   strips

1 tablespoon fresh tarragon leaves, chopped, or
   ½ teaspoon dried

2 tablespoons unsalted butter

¼ teaspoon salt

¼ teaspoon freshly ground black pepper

1. In a medium skillet, heat the olive oil over moderately high heat. Add the mushrooms and cook, stirring often, until they begin to brown, about 5 minutes. Add the onion and garlic, reduce the heat to moderately low and cook until the onion is softened, 3 to 5 minutes. Pour in the chicken broth, bring to a simmer and continue to simmer while you cook the pasta.

2. Bring a large saucepan of salted water to a boil. Add the rigatoni and cook, stirring occasionally, until *al dente*, tender but still slightly resistant to the bite, 10 to 12 minutes. Drain well and set aside in the saucepan in a warm spot.

3. Bring the mushroom mixture to a boil over moderately high heat. Add the artichokes, tuna, sun-dried tomatoes, tarragon and butter. Stir until heated through and the butter is melted, about 1 minute. Season the sauce with the salt and pepper. Pour over the rigatoni and toss to coat. Serve hot.

TUNA PESTO BAKE

▼▼▼▼▼

Basil, garlic and Parmesan cheese—the predominant flavors of a traditional pesto—are incorporated here into a creamy white sauce and tossed with pasta and canned tuna. The result is a spectacular do-ahead casserole. This rich, tasty dish can be prepared several hours in advance and baked shortly before serving.

MAKES 6 SERVINGS

½ cup walnut halves, finely chopped

2 tablespoons unsalted butter

2 tablespoons olive oil

2 medium garlic cloves, minced

¼ cup all-purpose flour

2 cups milk

1 pound medium pasta shells

2 (6⅛-ounce) cans solid white tuna in oil, drained

½ cup heavy cream

¼ cup finely chopped fresh basil

¼ teaspoon salt

½ teaspoon freshly ground black pepper

¼ cup plus 2 tablespoons grated Parmesan cheese

2 tablespoons plain dry bread crumbs

1. Place the finely chopped nuts in a dry medium skillet over moderate heat. Cook, stirring constantly, for about 3 minutes, until lightly toasted and fragrant. Transfer to a plate to cool.

2. In a medium saucepan, melt the butter in the oil over low heat. Add the garlic and cook, stirring, for 1 minute, or until fragrant but not browned. Increase the heat to moderate. Add the flour and cook, stirring, for about 2 minutes without browning. Gradually whisk in the milk about ¼ cup at a time. Bring to a boil, whisking, until smooth and thickened, about 2 minutes. Reduce the heat to low and simmer for 3 minutes longer, stirring often. Remove the white sauce from the heat.

3. Preheat the oven to 375°. Meanwhile, cook the shells in a large pot of boiling salted water until just tender, about 10 minutes. Drain the pasta well and stir into the white sauce. Add the tuna, cream, basil, salt, pepper, toasted chopped walnuts, and ¼ cup of the Parmesan cheese. Scrape into a 1½- to 2-quart soufflé dish or casserole. Sprinkle the remaining 2 tablespoons Parmesan cheese over the top.

4. Bake for about 45 minutes, until bubbly and golden brown on top. Let cool for 10 minutes before serving.

CREAMED CHIPPED
TUNA ON TOAST
▼▼▼▼▼

For a quick-to-prepare and satisfying dinner, serve this dish with a side of steamed frozen peas and a small salad.

MAKES 4 SERVINGS

3 tablespoons unsalted butter

3 tablespoons all-purpose flour

2 cups milk

4 slices of firm-textured white bread (feel free to
   substitute any kind of sliced bread.)

2 (6⅛-ounce) cans solid white tuna in oil, drained and
   flaked

Pinch of ground nutmeg

½ teaspoon freshly ground black pepper, or to taste

1. Melt the butter in a medium saucepan over moderately high heat. Stir in the flour and cook, stirring, for 2 minutes without browning. Gradually whisk in the milk. Reduce the heat to moderate and bring to a boil, whisking, stirring constantly, until the sauce is smooth and thickened, 3 to 5 minutes. Reduce the heat to low.

2. Toast the slices of bread. While the bread is toasting, stir the tuna, nutmeg and pepper into the white sauce and heat gently until warm.

3. To serve, halve the toast slices. Arrange 2 pieces on each of 4 plates. Spoon about ⅔ cup of the tuna mixture over each portion. Serve hot.

▼ THE TUNA FISH GOURMET ▼

TUNA STROGANOFF

▼▼▼▼▼

A spinoff on the classic beef dish. Serve tossed with lightly buttered noodles or over steamed white rice.

MAKES 4 SERVINGS

2 tablespoons unsalted butter
10 ounces medium mushrooms, thinly sliced
1 medium onion, finely chopped
1 garlic clove, minced
2 tablespoons all-purpose flour
¼ cup dry sherry
1 cup reduced-sodium chicken broth
1 cup sour cream
2 (6⅛-ounce) cans solid white tuna in oil, drained
¼ teaspoon sweet paprika
¾ teaspoon freshly ground black pepper
Salt

1. Melt 1 tablespoon of the butter in a medium skillet over moderately high heat. Add the sliced mushrooms and cook, stirring often, until browned, about 5 minutes. Transfer the mushrooms to a plate and set aside.

2. Reduce the heat to moderately low. Add the remaining 1 tablespoon butter. When melted, add the onion and garlic and cook, stirring occasionally, until translucent, about 3 minutes. Add the flour and cook, stirring, for 2 minutes, until pasty and dry but not browned. Stir in the sherry and cook until evaporated, about 1 minute. Gradually stir in the chicken broth and bring to a boil over moderately high heat, stirring until thickened. Reduce the heat and simmer 3 to 5 minutes.

3. Stir in the sour cream, tuna, paprika and pepper and stir until heated through, about 3 minutes. Do not boil. Season to taste with salt if desired. Serve over pasta or rice.

▼ THE TUNA FISH GOURMET ▼

TUNA BURGERS

▼▼▼▼▼

For a quick and satisfying meal, serve these burgers with a lettuce and tomato salad and, in summer, fresh corn on the cob.

MAKES 4 SERVINGS

2 (6⅛-ounce) cans solid white tuna in oil, drained and
    flaked
¼ cup cream cheese, softened
2 teaspoons fresh lemon juice
2 tablespoons mayonnaise
1 teaspoon freshly ground black pepper
¼ cup all-purpose flour
2 eggs
1 tablespoon minced fresh tarragon or 1 teaspoon dried
½ cup plain dry bread crumbs
¼ teaspoon salt
3 tablespoons unsalted butter
4 hamburger buns
Tartar sauce

1. In a medium bowl, combine the tuna, cream cheese, lemon juice, mayonnaise and ½ teaspoon of the pepper. Mix with a fork until blended. Dust your hands with the flour and form the tuna mixture into 4 patties about 3½ inches in diameter. Coat the patties well with the flour.

2. Beat the eggs in a small bowl until blended. In a medium bowl, toss together the tarragon, bread crumbs, salt and remaining ½ teaspoon pepper. Turn each tuna burger in the egg wash, then dredge in the seasoned bread crumbs to coat. Repeat the process for a double coating of crumbs.

3. Heat 1½ tablespoons of the butter in a large heavy skillet over moderate heat. Add the tuna burgers and cook for about 1½ minutes, until golden brown on the bottom. Flip the burgers, add the remaining 1½ tablespoons butter to the pan and cook for 1½ minutes longer, until browned on the second side. Transfer to the buns and serve immediately, with tartar sauce on the side.

TUNA TETRAZZINI

▼▼▼▼▼

Mushrooms and pasta in white sauce are the hallmarks of a tetrazzini, which is traditionally made with turkey, chicken or seafood. I've used tuna fish, or course, with spaghetti, and finished the dish with a crispy crumb topping.

MAKES 6 SERVINGS

4 tablespoons unsalted butter

1 pound small white mushrooms, quartered

1 large celery rib, finely chopped

1 small onion, finely chopped

¼ cup all-purpose flour

2 cups milk

1 (10½-ounce) can reduced-sodium chicken broth

3 (6⅛-ounce) cans solid white tuna in water, drained
   and flaked

¼ teaspoon salt

½ teaspoon freshly ground black pepper

½ pound spaghetti

1½ cups fresh white bread crumbs

3 tablespoons melted unsalted butter

1. Preheat the oven to 350°. Put a large saucepan of salted water on to boil over moderately high heat for cooking the pasta.

2. Melt 1 tablespoon of the butter in a heavy medium saucepan over moderately high heat. Add the mushrooms and cook, stirring occasionally, until the juices have evaporated and the mushrooms are nicely browned, about 5 minutes. Remove the mushrooms to a plate.

3. Melt the remaining 3 tablespoons butter in the same pan over moderately low heat. Add the celery and cook for 4 minutes, stirring occasionally. Stir in the onion and cook until the vegetables are softened and translucent, about 5 minutes.

4. Increase the heat to moderate, stir in the flour and continue to stir until pasty, about 1 minute, to cook the starch Gradually whisk in the milk and then the chicken broth. Bring to a boil and cook, stirring often, until thickened, 3 to 5 minutes. Stir in the tuna, salt, pepper and reserved mushrooms. Remove from the heat and cover to keep warm.

5. Cook the spaghetti in the saucepan of boiling water until *al dente*, tender but still slightly resistant to the bite, about 8 minutes. Drain well; do not rinse. Reheat the tuna and mushroom sauce if necessary. Stir the pasta into the sauce. Scrape the mixture evenly into a shallow 12-by-8-inch glass baking dish. Sprinkle on the bread crumbs and drizzle the melted butter over the top. Bake for 20 minutes, or until the dish is hot throughout and the crumbs are golden.

TUNA À LA KING

▼▼▼▼▼

A versatile dish that is wonderful over rice, toast, puff pastry shells or pasta (fettuccine is my favorite here). This recipe can also be used as the filling for tuna pot pie, as suggested in the recipe that follows.

MAKES 6 SERVINGS

4 scallions, chopped

4 tablespoons unsalted butter

¼ cup plus 2 tablespoons all-purpose flour

3 cups milk

2 large carrots, cut into ¼-inch dice

1 cup fresh or thawed frozen peas

8 asparagus spears, cut into ½-inch pieces

2 (6⅛-ounce) cans solid white tuna in oil, drained

½ cup finely diced pimiento

½ teaspoon salt

½ teaspoon freshly ground black pepper

1. Place the scallions and butter in a large saucepan over moderately low heat. Cook, stirring, until the scallions are softened, about 2 minutes. Add the flour and cook, stirring, for 1 to 2 minutes without browning. Gradually whisk in the milk. Bring to a boil, whisking until smooth and thickened, about 3 minutes. Reduce the heat to low and simmer for 4 minutes longer, stirring often. Remove from the heat. (The white sauce can be made up to a day ahead. Let cool completely; then cover and refrigerate.)

2. Bring a medium saucepan of water to a boil over moderately high heat. Add the carrots, peas and asparagus, and cook for 5 minutes; drain and rinse under cold running water. Drain well.

3. Reheat the white sauce, if necessary. Stir the tuna, pimiento, salt, pepper and cooked vegetables into the sauce. Cook over moderate heat, stirring gently, until hot, about 1 minute.

TUNA POT PIE
▼▼▼▼▼

Pot pies can be made in individual serving portions or in one large casserole. Homemade flaky pie pastry can be used instead of the puff pastry suggested here. If using a deep dish, make sure the filling is warmed through. Even though there is the pastry crust on top, I like to serve rice or noodles as well as a tossed salad on the side.

MAKES 4 TO 6 SERVINGS

8 ounces or half of a 17½-ounce box of frozen puff
   pastry (preferably all-butter), thawed but chilled
1 recipe Tuna à la King (page 130), warm or at room
   temperature
1 egg, beaten

▼ THE TUNA FISH GOURMET ▼

1. Preheat the oven to 400° Get out a 4- to 6-quart casserole or 4 individual 2-cup ramekins. With a rolling pin, roll out the pastry ⅛ inch thick. Using the bottom of the dish as a guide, cut a circle or circles 1 inch wider than the large dish and ½ inch wider than the smaller dishes with a pastry wheel or pizza cutter. With a small sharp knife, cut several slits near the center of each puff pastry disc(s) to act as a steam vent.

2. Spoon the tuna à la king into the casserole(s). Lightly but thoroughly brush the rim and a small portion of the top outer side of the dish(es) with the beaten egg. Carefully lay the pastry over the top(s), pressing to seal the overhanging pastry to the outer edge. Brush the top of the pastry with the remaining beaten egg; make sure the steam vents are not sealed together with egg by running the tip of the knife through them again.

3. Place the dish(es) on a large baking sheet and bake for 20 to 30 minutes, until puffed and golden on top and bubbly hot inside. Check the vents for steam as an indication.

▼ THE TUNA FISH GOURMET ▼

FRITTATA WITH TUNA, ZUCCHINI AND TOMATO

▼▼▼▼▼

During the months when tomatoes aren't at their best, substitute roasted or fresh red bell peppers. If you don't have a skillet with a flameproof handle, flip the frittata onto a large plate and slide it back into the skillet, instead of finishing the cooking under the broiler.

MAKES 4 SERVINGS

1 tablespoon mild olive oil

1 medium onion, halved, peeled and thinly sliced

1 medium zucchini (8 ounces), cut into ½-inch dice

½ teaspoon dried oregano

½ teaspoon freshly ground black pepper

¼ teaspoon salt

6 large eggs

1 (6½-ounce) can tuna in olive oil, drained and lightly
   flaked

4 ounces semisoft cheese, such as Italian Fontina or
   Jarlsberg, cut into ⅜-inch dice (about ¾ cup)
1 medium tomato, cut into ½-inch dice

1. Preheat the broiler. Heat the oil in a medium flameproof skillet, preferably cast-iron, over moderate heat. Add the onion and cook, stirring frequently, until limp, about 3 minutes. Stir in the zucchini, oregano, pepper and salt and cook, stirring occasionally, until the vegetables are soft, about 4 minutes.

2. In a medium bowl, beat the eggs and 1 tablespoon of water with a fork until blended. Pour the eggs into the skillet. Cook, stirring gently and constantly with a wooden spoon, until the eggs are half scrambled, 2 to 3 minutes.

3. Reduce the heat to low. Stir in the tuna, diced cheese and tomato. Smooth out the top of the frittata, cover and let cook for 3 minutes, or until set but very moist around the edges and on top.

4. Finish the frittata by broiling until slightly puffed, 1 to 2 minutes, or flip onto a dish as directed above and let cook for 1 minute longer, until firm but not dry Cut into 4 wedges and serve hot, warm or at room temperature.

TUNA BAKE WITH BROCCOLI, CHEDDAR AND POTATOES

▼▼▼▼▼

My friend Dot Stack loves this dish. She serves it to friends whenever she's planning an easy cozy dinner. Mixed greens tossed with a vinaigrette are great on the side, and a simple dessert, like brownies and ice cream, will complete the scene.

MAKES 4 TO 6 SERVINGS

1 bunch of broccoli, cut into 4-inch-long spears about
  ½ inch thick at the stem
2 tablespoons unsalted butter
3 tablespoons all-purpose flour
2 cups milk
1 teaspoon freshly ground black pepper
½ teaspoon salt
¼ pound extra-sharp white Cheddar cheese, crumbled
  (about 1 cup)

1½ pounds baking potatoes (3 large), peeled and very
   thinly sliced crosswise
1 cup heavy cream
2 (6⅛-ounce) cans solid white tuna in oil, drained and
   flaked

1. Bring a large saucepan of salted water to a boil over moderately high heat.
Add the broccoli spears and cook until barely tender, 3 to 5 minutes. Drain
and rinse under cold running water. Drain well.

2. In a medium saucepan, melt the butter over moderate heat. Add the flour
and cook, stirring, 2 minutes without allowing the flour to brown. Gradually
whisk in the milk. Bring to a boil, whisking until smooth and thick, about
2 minutes. Reduce the heat to low and simmer, stirring often, for 3 minutes.
Remove from the heat and stir in ½ teaspoon of the salt and the Cheddar
cheese. Set the cheese sauce aside. (The recipe can be made to this point up
to 1 day ahead. Wrap the broccoli and sauce separately and store overnight in
the refrigerator.)

3. Preheat the oven to 400° Butter a 9-inch square baking dish. Arrange the
potatoes in an even layer, overlapping the slices, on the bottom of the dish.
Pour the cream over the potatoes and season with the remaining ¼ teaspoon
salt and ½ teaspoon pepper. ▶

4. Sprinkle the tuna evenly over the potatoes, then arrange the broccoli spears in overlapping rows on top. Pour the reserved cheese sauce over all.

5. Cover the dish with the foil and bake for 30 minutes. Reduce the oven temperature to 300°, uncover and bake for 30 minutes longer. Let stand for about 10 minutes before serving.

WARM TUNA WITH LEMON CREAM

▼▼▼▼▼

One of the quickest hot tuna dishes, this is wonderful with a side of sautéed grated zucchini spiked with Parmesan cheese. Serve over steamed white rice or noodles.

MAKES 2 SERVINGS

2 tablespoons unsalted butter
2 tablespoons fresh lemon juice
⅔ cup heavy cream
1 teaspoon finely grated lemon zest
1 (6⅛-ounce) can solid white tuna in oil, drained and
　flaked
¼ teaspoon freshly ground pepper
Pinch of salt

1. In a medium saucepan, combine the butter and lemon juice. Cook over low heat until the butter is melted, about 2 minutes. Stir in the cream and heat gently until hot. Do not boil.

2. Just before you're ready to eat, stir in the lemon zest, tuna, pepper and salt and cook until heated through, about 1 minute. Serve immediately.

TUNA STRUDEL

▼▼▼▼▼

Rather than paper-thin strudel pastry, this savory version uses an easy cream cheese dough made in the food processor. Serve chilled pastry for a special-occasion luncheon.

MAKES 6 SERVINGS

PASTRY:

1 cup all-purpose flour

½ tablespoon dried thyme

½ teaspoon salt

¼ teaspoon freshly ground pepper

6 tablespoons cold unsalted butter, cut up

2 ounces cream cheese, cut up

1 egg yolk

2 tablespoons ice water

FILLING:

2 (6⅛-ounce) cans solid white tuna in water, drained
   and flaked

¼ cup mayonnaise

1 tablespoon fresh lemon juice

¼ cup finely chopped yellow bell pepper

¼ cup finely chopped red bell pepper

¼ cup finely chopped celery

¼ cup finely chopped cucumber

1 medium carrot, shredded

1 tablespoon minced fresh chives

2 tablespoons finely chopped red onion

1. Make the pastry: In a food processor, place the flour, thyme, salt and
pepper. Pulse several times to sift together. Add the cold butter and cream
cheese and process until mealy, about 8 seconds. Add half of the egg yolk,
reserving the other half for glazing, and the ice water and process until the
mixture barely begins to come together. Transfer to a work surface, gather the
dough and knead briefly to blend. Beat the reserved ½ egg yolk with 1
teaspoon of water; cover and refrigerate until ready to bake. Form the dough
into a disc, wrap and refrigerate for 30 minutes. ▶

2. While the dough is chilling, make the filling: In a medium bowl, combine the tuna, mayonnaise and lemon juice with a fork until well blended. Add the yellow and red bell peppers, the celery, cucumber, carrot, chives and red onion and toss to distribute. Set aside. Preheat the oven to 400°.

3. Lightly flour a work surface. Roll out the pastry into a 12-by-20-inch rectangle; trim evenly to 10 by 18 inches. Transfer to a large, ungreased baking sheet. Spoon the tuna mixture down the center of the length of the pastry, leaving a 1-inch border on the short ends.

4. Using a pastry brush dipped in water or wet fingertips, dampen the pastry around the perimeter. Fold the short ends up over the tuna mixture. Bring the long sides up and pinch them together in the center. Crimp the seam with a fork and your finger to seal. Lightly brush the strudel all over with the reserved egg wash, making sure to brush along the seam and ends so the filling will not leak out during baking. With a small sharp knife, cut 4 holes in the top near the seam for ventilation. Bake in the preheated oven for 30 minutes, until golden brown and bubbly. Let cool on a rack to room temperature, about 30 minutes. Refrigerate until chilled, 3 hours or overnight.

TOKYO TUNA

▼▼▼▼▼

This Asian-inspired dish can be whipped up in a flash. Serve over steamed aromatic rice, such as basmati or jasmine, or over soba noodles, which are made with buckwheat and are available in Asian markets.

MAKES 2 SERVINGS

2 teaspoons peanut oil
1 small garlic clove, minced
2 medium scallions, finely sliced
1 teaspoon minced fresh ginger
2 tablespoons soy sauce
Pinch of sugar
1 (6⅛-ounce) can solid white tuna in water, drained

1. Heat a heavy medium skillet over moderately high heat until almost smoking. Add the oil and tilt to coat the bottom of the pan. Add the garlic, scallions and ginger and stir-fry for 1 minute, until fragrant and golden.

2. Stir in the soy sauce, sugar and ⅓ cup water. Bring to a boil, add the tuna and cook, stirring, until heated through. Serve immediately over rice or soba noodles.

▼ THE TUNA FISH GOURMET ▼

TURKEY IN COLD
TUNA SAUCE
▼▼▼▼▼

Inspired by the classic Italian dish vitello tonnato—*cold, sliced roasted veal in a creamy tuna puree—this dish takes advantage of turkey leftovers to make a tasty and healthy substitute for the veal.*

MAKES 6 SERVINGS

1 (6½-ounce) can tuna in olive oil, oil reserved

2 anchovy fillets, rinsed (optional)

2 tablespoons white wine vinegar

1 tablespoon fresh lemon juice

2 tablespoons chopped parsley

½ teaspoon freshly ground black pepper

1½ cups mayonnaise

¼ cup capers, rinsed and drained

Salt (optional)

1½ pounds sliced roasted turkey or 6 sliced large
    cooked chicken breast halves, chilled

1. Place the tuna with its oil, the anchovies, vinegar, lemon juice, parsley and pepper in a food processor and process until relatively smooth, about 15 seconds. Scrape down the side of the bowl. Add the mayonnaise and 2 tablespoons of the capers, reserving the remaining capers for garnish. Pulse until just blended. Taste and season with salt to taste.

2. Arrange the sliced turkey on 6 individual plates. Spoon about ⅓ cup of the sauce over each serving and garnish each with 1 teaspoon of the reserved capers. Serve at room temperature or slightly chilled.

▼ THE TUNA FISH GOURMET ▼

INDEX

▼▼▼▼▼